RAPID WEIGHT LOSS HYPNOSIS

Lose weight naturally fast through meditation techniques, hypnosis, hypnotic gastric band and improve mindful eating.

by Laura White

D1569413

1

2

against the publisher for any reparation, damages, or financial loss due to information provided here, directly or indirectly. The author owns the copyright that the publisher does not own.

The information herein is provided for educational purpose exclusively and is universal. The presentation of the data is without contractual agreement or any kind of warranty assurance.

All trademarks inside this book are for clarifying purposes only and are possessed by the owners themselves, not allied with this document.

Disclaimer

All erudition supplied in this book are specified for educational and academic purpose only. The author is not in any way in charge for any outcomes that emerge from using this book.

Constructive efforts have been made to render information that is both precise and effective, however the author is not to be held answerable for the accuracy or use/misuse of this information.

Foreword

I will like to thank you for taking the very first step of trusting me and deciding to purchase/read this life-transforming book. Thanks for investing your time and resources on this product.

I can assure you of precise outcomes if you will diligently follow the specific blueprint I lay bare in the information handbook you are currently checking out. It has transformed lives, and I strongly believe it will equally transform your own life too. All the information I provided in this *Do It Yourself* piece is easy to absorb and practice.

Table of Contents

INTRODUCTION

The power of Hypnosis is the mind. But the power of the mind is underrated. The mind can choose to manage the body's breathing rate, heartbeat, high blood pressure, weight status, and others. Many people have made powerful claims about how someone can be discreetly hypnotized to do things.

This book will talk specifically about how Hypnosis can help to fight weight loss and make you keep fit. The principles explained in the book consist of how Hypnosis relates to mind control and taking a look at the so-called "myths" of Hypnosis.

There was a period in time when the thought of dropping weight didn't occur in our society, individuals consumed what their mothers prepared for breakfast and they went to work. The difference between the then society and today's society is that work was not behind a computer screen, but mostly on their feet in the fields or on a factory floor. People mostly worked physically because that was the only method to work, in reality, that's why it was called work! It was commonly during this time around that individuals could eat anything they desired since they were melting a lot more calories than what they ate.

Like all good things, that period has passed and the modern technology of today's world has left us in one condition-- an overweight one. Our life styles have transformed so dramatically and our comforts have boosted significantly. As they say, every development has its thorn and for our society our desire to have comfortable lives and to work less has started to show around the waist.

The bad aspect of this is that the more weight you acquire, the more dangerous it becomes. Additional weight spells health problem, whether it is in the kind of diabetic issues or a heart problem, it's bound to appear if you don't throw down the gauntlet. You have to be aggressive in weight gain and you need to work it off till it gets to a level where you have full control. It is not necessarily about being toned and sculpted, yet at a weight that is not harmful. You can work with the abs later on, today you simply require to lose some extra body fat. As society understands what is taking place and that we are overweight in its entirety, individuals are trying to play catch up and work from behind. They are attempting to lose weight and live a much healthier way of living.

This book is your overview to shedding that initial ten extra pounds that we all battle with.

It's impressive what little changes in your life can add up to you losing ten pounds and they all focus on eating right and getting your body in action.

CHAPTER ONE

What is Hypnosis?

Hypnosis is something we usually consider as a kind of entertainment but have you ever thought about hypnosis for weight-loss? It's trying to use hypnosis to deal with an issue as serious as weight problems, but probably it's not even as ridiculous as it sounds. Hypnosis for weight-loss is definitely an appealing idea - it offers people a reasonably simple way out of their weight problem, by stopping their yearnings for food at the source.

One problem with weight-loss through hypnosis is the same issue that afflicts other weight reduction solutions.

Many scams exist out there, and the individuals behind them will not hesitate about trying to collect your money for the sale of a product that does not do anything at all. Hypnosis has the very same problem. You might be able to trust some claims about hypnosis weight reduction treatment, however, there are just as lots that have lots of lies.

If hypnosis for weight-loss treatment declares it can help you to lose some insane number of pounds in a couple of weeks or similar exaggerations, it's pretty safe to bet that it's a scam. If you find claims that state that hypnosis can totally alter the way the mind works to prevent eating, they're probably deceptive.

At the point of sleeping or waking up from sleep, your mind goes through the various phases of brainwave activity. Bata is the position you are now if you are not daydreaming that is. The waves are quick. Just under that awareness is Alpha. The waves are slower, and you are awake; however, in a modified state of awareness. Have you ever driven your vehicle and you are concern just at your exit questioning where you were? Yes, you have your mind attached to the Alpha state while driving. This is the same thing your mind does while in hypnosis. Keep in mind while driving your automobile you remained in control, you didn't hit anything, its the same with hypnosis. Under Alpha comes Theta, you're not sleeping but headed towards sleep. Then you are asleep, that is called Delta. When you get up you go through those brainwave states in reverse.

Now that we comprehend how our minds work let's start discussing hypnosis. Hypnosis is the bypass of the crucial aspect in the conscious mind and the establishment of accepting discerning thoughts. Note the meaning doesn't state anything about relaxation or surrendering your control? Hypnosis is a natural state.

Ever read a book and sort of slip off elsewhere in your mind? If you said yes to any of these questions, then you've been hypnotized before. Individuals often say it's like daydreaming; however, that may not be exactly correct. Daydreaming is typically when your mind is thinking about something, thinking about being on a boat or in some other particular circumstance or scene. I know when I'm driving my vehicle, and I slip into that "Zone" my mind is practically blank, I'm not considering anything. You can go into hypnosis by gazing at a dot on the wall.

The truth remains that hypnosis can help you lose weight. Hypnosis is more science than magic, all it truly is when a person gets in a state of deep, relaxed concentration in which they are more suggestible.

A session of hypnosis will not make you into some sort of robot that's immune to yearnings and programmed not to overindulge. What it can do, however, is make a person more

15

likely to follow a correct dietary strategy. The effects are entirely psychological. Hypnosis can't "persuade" your body to accelerate weight-loss, it can only implant the concept in your brain that maybe you do not require to eat that 2nd piece of cake.

People looking for hypnotic services to weight loss should be especially careful of group hypnosis sessions. In order to work, hypnosis needs to be customized specifically to the person getting it. Group sessions plainly will not work, as the therapist can not connect with any single person on his or her own. You should also be warned against hypnosis cassettes or videos, as they share this same issue.

Hypnosis for weight reduction is a really tempting thought. If you can train your mind to minimize your yearnings and increase your self-discipline, you'll be well on your way to dropping weight. The significant point to have in mind is to be cautious and study all the alternatives before you buy an item or see a hypnotherapist, or else you may end with nothing at all.

Have you attempted hypnosis before? If NO, then this section of the book will tell you a little regarding hypnosis and what you may expect to experience, just to put your mind at rest and assist you in getting the most from this astonishingly effective kind of help.

"Hypnosis" emerges from a Greek word "Hypnos" which means sleep (you might not be sleeping).

In 1891 the British Medical Association voted in favour of the usage of hypnosis in medication; however it was not authorized till 1955, years later! It has helped to solved numerous problem such as; Weight control, cigarette smoking addiction, motivation to workout, enhancing research study habits, managing worried habits, and developing a healthy self-esteem are a few of the conditions that can be influenced, with positive outcomes, through healing hypnosis.

Now let me put a few of your possible concerns to rest and to eliminate some concerns you might have from your mind.

Hypnosis can just take place if you want it to. If you enable it, you can just be hypnotised. I can not simply approach you and hypnotise you without you understanding about it allowing it. This indicates that hypnosis is safe for everyone that wishes to use it to assist with weight loss and more!

Hypnosis is not some kind of magical mind control that robs you of your will or ability to make educated choices. Hypnosis is a transformed state of awareness, that makes you more susceptible to tips and instructions that can help you in making positive behavioural and physical changes such as weight control, cigarette smoking addiction, motivation to exercise, improving study routines, controlling worried practices and establishing a healthy self-confidence. It is just one of lots of approaches of therapy that can assist in a large range way, for a wide variety of physical and behavioural problems.

Under hypnosis, you can not be forced into doing anything versus your will or your ethical code. It takes place during the session that requires your instant attention; you will still be able to deal with it.

Throughout your hypnosis session, you might not believe that you remain in a hypnotic trance, but you will most likely have the chance to observe your focus narrow and your breathing slow as you start to enter the alpha and relax state. Alpha is a level of awareness or a hypnotic trance, which is one level listed below being wide-awake or fully conscious, referred to as the Beta state of consciousness. In the Alpha state, you might become a hundred times more susceptible to suggestion and instructions as a person ultimately conscious, or the Beta state.

To clearly describe the benefits of the Alpha state, envision, there is a pipeline going directly through the conscious into the subconscious mind. In the subconscious, the recommendations are 200 times more likely to be efficient than the things we actually tell ourselves in our normal Beta state. Hypnosis is a way to reorder the mind's associations into more favorable and healthy instructions.

In some cases with weight control, we have to delve a little deeper into discovering what enhanced or necessitated the weight gain, and this might take additional sessions, but the outcomes at the end will justify investing this additional time. An American Health Magazine study found that psychoanalysis provided a 38% recovery after 600 sessions, behaviour treatment provided a 72% recovery after 22 sessions, and hypnosis provided an amazing 93% healing after six sessions. As you can see, hypnosis has been shown to very effective and safe at assisting you reach your goals rapidly.

Hypnosis is a typical state, it's something that you experiences every day. For instance, when you are absorbed by an excellent movie or a TV-show then you are in a hypnosis state. If you have ever been driving to work or the shop and you questioned how you got there because your mind was considering a thousand other things, you've experienced hypnosis. If you've ever been in the "zone" where you are focused on the job at hand and nothing else, you've been in hypnosis. If you've ever found yourself day-dreaming, you remained in a hypnosis. Even when you are reading a good book, you can be so absorbed that you do not hear when someone speak with you. By then, your brain gets into a different state - hypnosis. However, it isn't required to do things like watch movies or read excellent books. It can also be boring things, which put you in a hypnotic state, as an unexciting lecture. When someone talk with a monotonous voice it can be hard to remain focused. Possibly you begin to dream about something more interesting - that is likewise hypnosis.

Simply keep in mind that you might be aware of whatever I say throughout the session and that's OKAY since you are still in hypnosis, you can constantly bring yourself right back to the waking Beta condition or state by opening your eyes or taking time to count "ONE-TWO-THREE" in your mind, and above all, always be in control.

Why Consider Hypnosis?

Hypnosis is frequently used in places of hazardous medication to deal with a variety of ailments. But what is hypnosis used to treat? Hypnosis can be used as a single treatment or in conjunction with other treatments.

History of Hypnosis

Hypnosis has existed as an approach of accessing the unconscious and allowing the unconscious to help the mind to achieve the changes and benefits desired, as long as we wish to change a habit. These conducts would not have been called hypnosis, but hypnotic not until Braid in 1842.

In the Ebers Papyrus, a treatment was discussed in which the physician placed his hands on the head of the patient and declaring superhuman curative powers offered forth with uncommon remedial utterances which were recommended to the patients and which led to treatments.

In the 18th century, the most popular figure in the development of hypnosis was Dr Frantz Anton Mesmer (1734-1815), an Austrian physician who used magnets and metal frames to carry out "passes" over the client to eliminate "obstructions" (causes of illness) in the magnetic forces in the body and to induce a trance-like state. In 1784, the Marquis de Puysegur a trainee of Dr Mesmer found how to lead a patient into a deep hypnotic trance state called "somnambulism", using relaxation techniques. The term "somnambulism" is still extensively used amongst hypnotherapists today in referral for a deep hypnotic trance state and sleep-walking. This method was used for lots of following years by surgeons in France consisting of Dr. Recamier who carried out the first recorded operation without anesthesia in 1821. The Marquis de Puysegur described three main works of this deep hypnotic trance state or somnambulism.

In 1841 a Scottish optometrist, Dr James Braid (1775 - 1860) found by an incident that a private fixating on an object could quickly reach a hypnotic trance state without the help of the mesmeric result endorsed by Dr Mesmer. He released his findings, refuted Mesmer's work and erroneously called his discovery "hypnotherapy" based on the Greek word "Hypnos" which implies "sleep". This was a wrong choice as hypnosis is not sleeping, nevertheless, the name has stayed, and mesmerism became hypnotherapy.

During Braid's research study on hypnosis he formed the following ideas, the majority of which still stand today:

1) That in a competent hand, there is no great risk associated with hypnotic treatment, and neither exists pain or discomfort.

2) That an excellent research study would be needed to understand a number of theoretical principles relating to hypnosis thoroughly.

3) That hypnosis is a powerful tool which must be entirely restricted to qualified experts.

4) That although hypnotism was capable of treating numerous illness for which there had formally been no treatment, it, however, was no panacea and was just a medical tool which ought to be used in combination with other medical

information, drugs, treatments, etc., in order to treat the client appropriately.

Sigmund Freud (1856-1939), the father of psychoanalysis, used hypnosis in his early work however became disillusioned by the principle. There is a belief that he did not have the determination for hypnosis and was not an excellent hypnotist. He became associated with hypnosis between1883-1887 and practised for some time and, in 1885 Freud spent some time with Charcot, and was really amazed. He likewise translated into German Bernheim's De la Suggestion.

In Vienna, Freud and his buddy Joseph Breuer used hypnosis successfully in psychotherapy and 1895, they produced their traditional 'Studies in Hysteria' Freud had checked out Nancy in 1889, and this visit had encouraged him of the 'effective psychological processes which nonetheless remain concealed from the consciousness of males'. He found the 'favourable transference' when a female client he had awakened from hypnosis tossed her arms around his neck. On this Freud composed 'I was modest enough not to attribute the event to my own alluring personal attraction, and I felt that I had now grasped the nature of the mysterious aspect that was at work behind hypnotism'.

Another precursor of modern-day hypnosis and self-advancement was Dr. Emile Coué (1857 - 1926) who, at the end of the 19th century, happened to be a believer in auto-suggestion and in the role of the hypnotherapist as a facilitator of change and healing using the total involvement of the client in the hypnosis process. By 1887 Coué was establishing the theory of auto-suggestion, which is maybe the very first-time ego-strengthening (a mainstay of traditional occult and shamanistic practices) was used by the modern scientific community. He thought in the value of the creativity in directing the will of a person and performed experiments to study how making suggestions to individuals altered their actions. His well-known self-help declaration: "Day by day in every method I am improving and better", is still used in the majority of self-improvement treatments.

1. Coue's Laws of Suggestion: The Law of Concentrated Attention - "Whenever attention is focused on an idea over and over once again, it spontaneously tends to understand itself."

2. The Law of Reverse Action - "The more one tries to do something, the less possibility one has of success"

3. The Law of Dominant Effect - "A more powerful emotion tends to replace a weaker one."

Coue believed that he did not recover people himself but simply facilitating their own self-healing and he understood the significance of the topic's involvement in hypnosis, a forerunner of the belief that 'There isn't such thing as hypnosis, only self-hypnosis.' Maybe his most famous idea was that imagination is always more effective than the will. For example, if you ask somebody to stroll along with a slab of wood on the flooring, they can generally do it without wobbling.

Myths of Rapid Weight Loss and Fast Dieting

1. Bad and Good Hypnosis

There is good, bad, and so-so hypnosis. Truly there is a load of crap out in the hypnosis world today. However, there is some good value indirect hypnosis as far as efficiency and being up to date.

Be really conscious because many hypnosis hucksters are offering "hypnotic snake oil" items such as low-rate subliminal messages and pseudo-spirituality things.

2. Only mental weaklings can be hypnotized/I can not be hypnotized.

Perhaps you have heard that "wise" people can not be hypnotized. Many people do not find that sort of thing to be very pleasant, and so they merely do not enter into hypnosis. It is that basic.

On the other hand, when you truly get to experience being masterfully and gently directed into a state of deep relaxation and focus, you will understand that you can, in reality, be hypnotized. In reality, anyone with sound mental professors and a sensible quantity of intelligence can be hypnotized. Fact be told, experience shows that people who are smart and have an innovative mind make the very best hypnosis subjects/clients because they can effectively "think outside the box" and do not limit their imaginations about what is possible for them.

3. Hypnosis is incline control/you are not the hypnotist's puppet.

The only individual who has outright control over your mind is you. A therapist can not make you do something you are not going to do. Strange newspaper article, stage hypnotists, and people who do not understand much about hypnosis have promoted this misconception for far too long.

That being stated, an individual can use hypnosis and persuasion strategies (both for good and for bad purposes) to cause another person to end up being more willing to do what they say and accept their suggestions. Eventually, though, everyone has the power to make his/her own decisions (even under hypnosis). A hypnotist can not require anyone to do anything against his/her will (including go against their morals) unless such individual is happy to do so in the first place.

Generally speaking, the therapist acts as a guide to lead you into a relaxed and focused state and uses mentally sound hypnotic techniques to help you make changes or experience particular things that you wish to experience.

4. Hypnosis is not sleep.

Because of this myth, people who attempt hypnosis for the first time frequently come out of it a little dissatisfied. They say things like, "I might hear whatever you said" or "I seemed like I could open my eyes and leave if I wanted to." In truth, when you remain in hypnosis, you can be conscious of your environment. Hypnotists typically use the word "SLEEP!" as a command to put somebody into hypnosis. This is basically because sleep is mostly used as a metaphor for helping somebody go into hypnosis.

5. You can not get "stuck" in hypnosis.

Nobody has ever gotten stuck in hypnosis. The major reason an individual would stay in hypnosis is because it feels wonderful to be so relaxed and focused,. The worst thing that would take place if the hypnotist left or suddenly died while the individual was in hypnosis is that the hypnotized individual would probably drop off to sleep and wake up feeling truly great.

6. Hypnosis is not amnesia.

You will not forget everything that took place while you were in hypnosis. Keep in mind; hypnosis doesn't necessarily refer to sleep. You are not unconscious while you are in hypnosis.

7. You will not reveal your deep, dark secrets in hypnosis.

You are in control of your own mind and will be even when you remain in hypnosis. You won't reveal anything you do not desire others to know unless you want to. Hypnosis can, nevertheless, be used as a method to assist individuals deal and check out with those things that they would not usually desire to speak about under regular scenarios. This is always done with the individual's consent and usually in the context of hypnotherapy.

8. You will not end up being another person.

You will always be yourself when you are in hypnosis. That being stated, a hypnotherapist can use hypnosis to assist another individual in exploring what it would resemble to "end up being" another individual. This is generally done so that the subject/client can experience what it would be like to have the traits that the individual they are "becoming" has (for example, self-confidence). The hypnotized person can then bring this quality back with them into their character when they come out from being in hypnosis.).

Well, if you wish to be hypnotized, I hope this clears up any mistaken beliefs you might have had about hypnosis. You have also been provided with answers to give people to help stop their fears and clear up their misconceptions about hypnosis.

Categories of Hypnosis

Hypnosis has been made use of for centuries as a tool to surprise, impress and to help cure and treat. The concepts of hypnosis remain the same for or any approach; however, there are different routes to accomplish it. The type of hypnosis used normally is reliant on the result that is needed.

- **Conventional Hypnosis**

Conventional hypnosis is the classic design of hypnosis and has been around for a long time. It is the version conducted by a therapist who puts the subject into a deep hypnotic trance and then directs them by using ideas and commands. Stage hypnotism uses this method.

The conventional hypnosis method has been much maligned and mocked over the years mainly unjustified, but regrettably, a few of the criticism is right. Making use of fake hypnosis using plants and performers has undermined the real conventional hypnosis technique. When appropriately applied, it is a reliable and essential tool which can be very useful.

- **Hypnotherapy**

Using hypnosis to promote healing or positive advancement in any way is understood as hypnotherapy. Hypnotherapy can likewise be used to control the sensations of pain, and hypnosis has been used to perform surgery on completely mindful patients who would be in obvious pain if not for the usage of hypnosis.

Hypnosis can be used to help individuals. With psychological issues, such as anxiety, hypnotherapy can be exceptionally reliable. Fears, dependencies and all sort of false ideas can be selectively reprogrammed and control negative forms of emotions. Hypnosis, as made use of in hypnotherapy, can also have tangible results, the most common is stopping of pain by allowing surgical procedures to be undertaken without the damage and threats related to anaesthesia.

Hypnotherapy normally uses extremely light hypnosis, not the deep trance state used in the traditional type. The essential point of the hypnotherapy is that the patient should remain totally focused on the treatment and listening to the words the therapist is saying.

- **Self Hypnosis/Auto Hypnosis**

Hypnosis and self-hypnosis are comparable. The hypnotherapist is merely the auto that assists the subject into a trance, however, it is the subject that processes the information, but the outcome is the very same.

Self-hypnosis can be used in an enormous means to hypnotherapy and is efficient in conquering mental issues, fears, stress and dependencies. It is typically used just to promote a state of deep relaxation.

- **NLP Hypnosis**

The NLP approach is still commonly used; nevertheless, it is now more widely used as a self-assistance tool to assist and promote the sensations of a well being. This method has a rapid growth in popularity and is being used by specialists for clients, service specialists, life coaches and self-help courses.

NLP hypnosis is used to deal with psychological or behavioural problems or just to enhance one's sense of well being. It is a fantastic tool for inspiration and enhancing self-confidence.

- **Ericksonian Hypnosis**

This hypnosis technique has several names, secret hypnosis, covert hypnosis, black ops hypnosis, instant hypnosis, conversational hypnosis. This method uses regular discussion and promotes hypnotic induction without the subject being conscious that it is taking place.

Ericksonian hypnosis or conversational hypnosis was begun by Dr Milton H. Erickson (a hypnotherapist). Erickson effectively mastered the use of language after being ill with polio, keeping him contained to bed for numerous years. During this time, he refined how to use typical discussion to induce hypnotic states without the subject understanding.

This of hypnosis can be used on those who are doubtful about hypnotherapy or more traditional hypnosis and has been stated to be more efficient on those who are more doubtful.

This technique or method can be used on those who are sceptical about hypnosis or who are unaware that they are being hypnotised. The use of hypnotic language and hypnosis strategies within the normal conversation can cause trance really rapidly.

This hypnosis technique was initially established as a hypnotherapy strategy, but it has actually ended up being more used by daily people in everyday lives. The strategy permits the individual to take more control of their lives and use these techniques to help them in many daily scenarios. The process is reasonably easy, but it will take time to master the technique.

Importance of Hypnosis For Women

Hypnosis can help individuals handle:

- Labour and childbirth.
- Irritable Bowel Syndrome discomfort.
- Post-op surgery bleeding and pain.
- Dental treatment recovery.
- Migraine headaches.
- Chemotherapy nausea/vomiting.
- Weak body immune systems.
- High blood pressure.
- Skin illness.
- Asthma.
- Negative behaviors like eating conditions, smoking cigarettes, drug abuse, bedwetting.
- Anxiety disorders, stress.
- Atopic and psoriasis dermatitis.
- Fears.

Hypnosis is used to help relax an individual, permitting them to end up being much more relaxed and comfortable. A person having chronic pain will reach a new level of relaxation after a hypnotherapy treatment. This new state of relaxation will assist them in coping with anxiety, avoid problems at work and at home, and help them better cope with the pain in general.

Hypnosis works much better for some people than for others. The individual must be motivated for the treatment to work. It is likewise essential to the success of hypnotherapy for the individual to be prepared to effectively handle the suggestions that come out of the session.

With hypnosis, there are choices. A consultation with a skilled hypnotherapist will help you identify the technique that is best for you. Before we consider what it can and can't do for us let's understand what self-hypnosis is. If you have ever gone to see a hypnotherapist, they might have informed you that all hypnosis is self-hypnosis. What this actually means is that no one can make you go into hypnosis without your approval or cooperation.

Absolutely nothing might be even more from the fact. Hypnosis is a natural state of mind that we all participate in numerous times a day. At any time your attention is so focussed that you are not conscious of what is going on around you, you remain in a hypnotic state. Whether it's watching television or reading or playing, whenever we slip out of today and dive into our minds and where our attention is focussed, we remain in a state of hypnosis.

Of course, when we discuss self-hypnosis in a healing sense, we are not talking about these experiences. We are speaking about a deliberate procedure where we take our attention off of our current environments and put ourselves in a modified state of mind for a particular purpose.

How do we do self-hypnosis?

There are as many ways to do self-hypnosis as there are individuals, but for this book, I will describe a reliable but basic way that anyone can do.

The first important thing you wish to do is find a peaceful place where you will not be interrupted. Give yourself a good time. Shut off your phone and ask the kids to be peaceful and entertain themselves for this time. In an emergency, though, know that you will quickly be stimulated and go back to regular waking awareness, without difficulty.

Get comfortable, whether sitting or lying down. If you like, you can have soft music in the background. There are many recordings of meditative music that are ideal for self-hypnosis. Some people use the music to take them deeper into relaxation.

Now focus on your breathing. Enjoy your breath going in and out of your nose. Feel the air going into your body. See your tummy fluctuate. Often the breathing workout is accompanied by the idea "Breathe in relaxation and calm and breathe our tension and tension".

You can also use relaxation to bring you down into an unwinded state of deep harmony and calm. Imagine the muscles around your eyes, starting to relax and go limp. Then take that feeling up to the top of your head. Feel all the muscles in your neck, head and face let unwind and go. Use this strategy to go all the method down your whole body, unwinding and relaxing all the way down.

Use words in your mind like "deeper and deeper into relaxation" "going all the way down" "calm tranquil relaxation" etc., as you breathe and feel all the tension moving out of your muscles.

Counting in reverse is another excellent way to take yourself deeper into relaxation. "10 decreasing, ... 9 twice as relaxed as before, ... 8 still going down ... and so on".

Everybody has a distinct experience as they go into hypnosis. Pay attention to your senses, and see how you will experience hypnosis. At this moment a lot of people will ask, "What's the distinction in between self-hypnosis and meditation?"

Meditation is a good practice for clearing your mind

Hypnosis is comparable because you may unwind and view your breathing, but that is where the resemblances end. Hypnosis has a particular intention connected to it, so rather than being clear, your mind is particularly active, although in a different way than your regular state of consiousness.

You will have to go into hypnosis deliberately. If the reason you are using hypnosis is for stress relief, for example, you may hold the intent of 'I am calm and relaxed throughout my day.

Imagination plays a large part in hypnosis. Envisioning the result you desire assists to implant the concept into your subconscious mind. When the concept remains in your subconscious mind, it ends up being a part of your daily life.

When you think of or imagine something enough, your subconscious mind will include it in your life. It becomes a part of you when you go into self-hypnosis with a particular work in mind and repeat that intention.

When you are in a state of hypnosis that you have control of, you will observe that, this belongs to your mind that stays in control at all times. It is that part of your mind that will repeat the objective. It will also bring you out of hypnosis at the agreed-upon time.

To come out of hypnosis, you may say to yourself, "I will now count from number one to five, and on the count of five, I will open my eyes and return to regular waking consciousness." Now count ... "1, turning up slowly ..., 2, feeling refreshed and rested and energetic ..., 3, feeling my body back in the room ..., 4, remembering every advantageous thing I have said to my subconscious mind today ..., five, all the way up, eyes open.".

Keep in mind that when you offer yourself a recommendation to repeat it a couple of times to truly get it into your mind. It might take a couple of times and a couple of days or weeks to see the changes in your life, but they will come if you actually do this treatment as described. Now I can hear you asking, "if I can do this all on my own, why would I go to a hypnotherapist?"

Here's the answer:

The word hypnosis and hypnotherapist have a significant difference. One is a state of mind and the other is therapy.

You can do a lot of good with self-hypnosis. There are several things you can do with self-hypnosis. There is one extremely crucial thing you can not do with self-hypnosis, and that is treatment.

A hypnotherapist makes use of therapeutic tools while the customer is in a state of hypnosis to make changes in their lives. It is not possible for somebody in hypnosis to ask questions and dig much more in-depth and use the tools required to discover the root of an issue or engage themselves with their inner kid in a healing method.

Self-hypnosis is extremely beneficial for stress reduction and other associated problems. For a healing experience, it is vital to have a hypnotherapist to deal with for the purpose of getting to the root of an issue and finding solutions.

When trying to find a hypnotherapist, discover someone with whom you feel comfy with. Ensure they have the training to do the job. If possible, check their qualifications. Any governmental company does not control hypnotherapy so anyone can hang a shingle and call themselves a hypnotherapist. Make sure the individual you are dealing with is correctly trained and expert in their service practice. It is a lot better to take your time in choosing the right hypnotherapist beforehand than you learn later on that you slipped up.

Some True Facts About Hypnosis

Some just imagine the zombie-like hypnotic trances in the movies we see from Hollywood! Others may have appeared hypnosis used to the typical areas such as dropping weight and giving up smoking cigarettes.

But it might surprise a number of you reading this that hypnosis has been certified by the American Medical Association for use in healthcare facilities since the late 1950s! And every week, it appears as though there are new findings and outcomes from new studies showing the effectiveness of hypnosis.

I know you'll find it mind-opening and definitely quite fascinating! So, let's enter it, shall we?

- "Hypnotherapists have special powers!"

Don't be afraid! They can certainly provide some powerful results; however, it is not as cape and dagger or supernatural as all those old Hollywood movies would have us think!

Therapists do not have any special powers. They just have the knowledge and experience to help put you into an intense state of relaxation, and then provide the best kind of message to your inner mind, which puts thought into actions!

- "Hypnosis just deals with weak-minded people!".

It is those who can focus and have a more creative mind that gets the best outcomes with hypnosis.

That's because all hypnosis is self-hypnosis. And those individuals with higher focus and imagination get much more powerful results with that procedure and skillset.

Hypnosis has likewise been used by thousands worldwide to improve confidence and self-confidence, release dependencies, release when crippling fears and phobias, finally lose that weight, stop smoking cigarettes, enhance mental capacity, and the list goes on.

CHAPTER TWO

Hypnosis and Weight Loss Meditation To Burn Fat

Are you tired of being heavy. You've attempted almost every new dietary idea, agonizing exercise program and tried night trend diet plan but it seems nothing has worked. You still can't appear to reduce weight, and you're starting to run out of options.

However close your eyes and picture this! Imagine being able to easily drop weight without challenging diets and agonizing exercises.

Imagine accelerating your metabolism naturally without side effects or unsafe drugs. And envision sensation blissfully gorgeous about your body and having the size self esteem you've always longed for in the process.

How does meditation help you lose weight?

It's a terrific question! And only the science of spirituality and the soul can answer it. The truth is, meditation re-wires your brain and lots of scientists are now finding how rest affect the brain. For instance, "lessons discovered" in a meditative state seem to be far more effective than those taken in throughout common states.

This means, mantras or affirmations about weight loss for example, that are processed by the meditative mind appear to "snap a switch" in your internal electrical wiring that regulate how fast your body burns fat.

Many cultural and religious customs that practice meditation have very low incidences of the physical issues we deal with in the West including much lower occurrence of weight problems. (and the REAL reason why many monks and "Zen" practitioners do not have the "buddha stubborn belly" as most core meditators are in perfect shape.

In walking meditation, you make use of the physical movement of your body as the object of your concentration and mindfulness. You bring your awareness to every physical feeling that occurs while walking.

When you just woke up, do you really need to relax more? Think about it- what is the average morning routine out there? Wake up and hit the snooze button a lot, jump out of the bed, probably shower, get some white bread toast and a triple shot of espresso as you dress and run out the door so you aren't late for work. Now, is that really calming? And is that actually a great way to begin the day? If you start the day running around like a chicken with its head cut off, what would the rest of your day be like? I find that a relaxing morning routine really helps get the day off on the right foot.

Being mindful is the best thing you can do first thing in the morning. It's time that you can spend alone. It makes you feel much better in the morning and it keeps you feeling good. It gives you energy as helps to clear your mind like nothing else. It makes you feel good about your day and your self, as it's undeniably a positive thing to do for yourself, it wakes up your whole body while keeping your mind clear and warming up your focus.

Habits and routines can help you grow yourself. The way you start your day is important to your state of mind. Here are five morning routines that can help you start every day in a positive state.

1. **Meditation**: Morning meditation sets the tone throughout the day. This will help you be more focused, content, and optimistic. Your mind has a predisposition to move from one thought to another. One of the benefits of meditation is the ability to distract from common thought patterns, especially negative patterns. This can help you be in a state of compassion and proactivity rather than a reactive state. Book at least about ten minutes a day at dawn and be prepared to face the day clearly.

2. **Warm up your neurons**: Your morning routine will greatly influence this process. If you are a "snooze button," the routine of your mind will be slow. Fill your morning with brain stimulation and revive those neurons. Add fast paced and catchy music to your morning. Neurons love music, I enjoy a catchy classic while spending the morning. This brings my thinking patterns to a positive state and energizes my body. Try

adding different scents, your brain will connect you with all kinds of positivity.

3. **Calm down in gratitude**: During your morning routine, start listing things that you are grateful for. Throughout the day your mind will be focused on the wonders of life. You will return your state of mind to a state of positivity and start helping others to do the same. It will also reduce the stress level on your body and improve your overall health and quality of life.

4. **Keep yourself at a high level of achievement:** Start your day with the intention of putting your best and achieving greatness. At the first moment of awakening, before sight, sound or smell, you are capable of everything. Then your "world" is in a hurry and your routines and patterns begin. Having a good morning routine may be helpful, but in itself it is not enough. You must be responsible for your achievement. Keep a detailed diary of what you are grateful for and what you hope to accomplish that day, that week, that month, or that particular year. Start small and work your way up. You will train your mind to focus on

what works best for your passions and you will begin to understand what your vision of success will look like.

Using good morning routines will make you positive and motivated to go out and make your life a success. Remember that change happens at many moments in your life. First become the person you envision to be, and then the life you envisioned will take shape around you.

Exercise For the day

Take some moments to think about how much time your mindful morning routine will take and be alert as you don't want to feel rushed. Decide where your mindful morning routine will take place, Do you want to have a dedicated space just for this purpose or will you do it in a multi-purpose space? Do you wish to stay indoors or spend mindful morning time outdoors?

Why Nutrient-Richness Can Help You Lose Weight

The current scientific research clearly shows that successful weight-loss requires that we eat nutrient-rich foods. In large, across the country research studies that have consisted of both healthy-weight and overweight individuals, insufficient intake of minerals and vitamins has been consistently connected to greater body weights. Consuming couple of fresh vegetables and fruits leads not just to insufficient nourishment, however, has also been linked to weight problems. In research studies of obese kids trying to slim down, increased intake of nutrient-rich in vegetables has likewise been connected with much better weight loss success. New proof associates diet plans high in veggies, salads, and fruits and low in processed and refined foods with healthy weight because they consist of phytonutrients, useful substances discovered exclusively in fruits and veggies that have the power to assist keep us healthy and help the body maintain optimal, healthy weight. Salads, fruits, and vegetables are abundant in anti-oxidants, which we require if we desire to lose weight. Studies reveal that overweight individuals have higher levels of oxidative stress from an excess of free radicals and the absence of anti-oxidants. What is it about nutrient-richness that assists promote weight loss? Several elements are been included. Nutrient-rich World's Healthiest Foods supply our body with important nutrient support that allows our body to bring out its metabolic activities in an optimal way. Metabolic activities, such as the burning of undesirable fat (a procedure called betaoxidation), are best supported by a diet that is abundant in nutrients. Given that we only have a minimal amount of calories that we can consume if we want to slim down or maintain our weight and simultaneously take in an adequate range and amount of nutrients to preserve our health, we need to get as numerous nutrients as possible in comparison to the variety of calories we take in. Luckily, it's simple to do this by focusing on the nutrient-rich World's Healthiest Foods. Each day, we require numerous nutrients to remain healthy, and these nutrients should be supplied by the food we eat.

Low-Calorie Dessert And Treat Options

Everyone likes a little something sweet from time to time, especially when they've been behaving well on a low-calorie diet. Fruits are always a great sweet treat, and for those times when you 'd like something a little bit more special, we've added some choices that can be had for 100 calories or less.

Do not hesitate to indulge when you have a yearning, but make sure that you're restricting these treats to just within a day or fulfilling it more occasionally. It's still crucial to attempt to keep sugar intake to a minimum, even on non-fasting days, so that your body's insulin and glucose levels start to reach a healthier, more well-balanced state.

- Cider or Apple juice, 1/2 cup 60 calories

- Blueberries, 1 cup 85 calories

- Caramels, 2 pieces 80 calories

- Cherries, 1/4 cup dried 100 calories

- Chocolate milk, 1/2 cup 75 calories

- Chocolate pudding, 1 fat-free (4-ounce) container 60 calories

- Chocolate sandwich cookies, 2 100 calories

- Dark chocolate, 1 ounce 100 calories

- Figs, 2 80 calories

- Fruit yogurt, 1/2 cup fat-free mixed 90 calories Frozen yogurt, 1/2 cup fat free 95 calories

- Jelly beans, 20 small 90 calories

- Kiwis, 2 medium 95 calories

- Oatmeal cookies, 2 little 100 calories

- Pineapple, 1 cup fresh 75 calories

- Pomegranate juice, 2/3 cup 90 calories

- Prune juice, 1/2 cup 90 calories
- Strawberry sorbet, 1 small scoop 100 calories Vanilla low-fat frozen yogurt, 1 small scoop 90 calories
- Watermelon, 2 cups 90 calories.

CHAPTER THREE

Guided Meditation for Weight Loss

Weight Management

Weight management is a lot more than just slimming down. Managing your weight in a healthy way guarantees ideal health and lowers the risks that come with some diets.

As a result, handling your weight means getting right into an agreement on your own to consume healthy and balanced foods in the right quantities, exercising in an all-natural way and minimizing the excess body fat in your body.

Due to these particular reasons, weight management products are becoming equally as popular as weight-loss products. Ensuring you get the appropriate nourishment, correct exercise and removing dangerous fat on your body can in some cases feel like effort.

With such conflicting recommendations existing in the weight-loss industry, it can be difficult to know when the suggestions you are offered is correct for you, efficient and, in some cases, even safe!

Your Body Knows

We are all integrated in a similar method or the other members of the pet kingdom. As mammals we have the capability to naturally get to a balance with our atmosphere.

Since the foundation of our species, our bodies have actually been evolving slowly, yet intelligently, equally as our brains have.

Over numerous years advancement has created the finest working equipment known - you!

When you need to eat, your body allows you to know by sending signals to the mind that it is hungry.

Similarly when you eat your body knows when it is complete and sends out signals to your mind informing it so.

Many of the time we disregard these signals and go on consuming)!

When you discover to listen to your body it guides you naturally to perform activities, automatically, that maintain you in top physical conditioning!

Your Mind Often Ignores Your Body

When your body sends signals to the brain letting it know what it needs really commonly these signals are entirely overlooked.

An individual with a weight problem has actually just conditioned their mind to neglect their body!

Through mental replacing it is feasible to find out and reverse this scenario to deal with your body so you can achieve your all-natural, suitable weight.

Replacing The Mind

The human mind is the most powerful computer system known to Man. This bio-computer can computing incredibly hard mathematical equations in a split second (like the trajectory of a baseball and its rate as well as the required adjustments it should make in your muscular tissues to increase your batting arm to strike the round in exactly the appropriate location at specifically the right time).

Your brain, or a lot more properly your mind, is accountable for instantly regulating your heart rate, high blood pressure and all the other bodily features you take for granted, as well as directing your behaviours, actions and even your needs.

Your mind is a super-computer!

When you have access to a computer system that effective it's worth finding out exactly how to use it!

You see, all your automatic practices, beliefs, memories and psychological reactions are stored in the subconscious component of your mind.

Since your subconscious mind has actually been conditioned to hate workout, if you despise workout it is merely. If you like chocolate cake and despise carrots, it is just because your subconscious mind has been conditioned to believe carrots do not taste good while chocolate preferences fantastic,

Just as it is feasible to use hypnotherapy to remove anxieties and concerns it is equally as easy to use this effective mind device to alter your attitude to food and exercise!

You can in fact problem your mind to take pleasure in the preference of healthy and balanced food and crave it. Additionally you can also educate your mind to take pleasure in exercise!

Hypnotherapy

Hypnotherapy has actually long been the choice of mind tool for creating quick, effective and long-term modifications in attitude, outlook, practices and feedbacks.

Why? Because it works!

Using Hypnotherapy

It is feasible to make the life-altering modifications in perspective that you require to make in order to accomplish and maintain your ideal weight and body form.

Working with the appropriate hypnotherapy program it is feasible to recondition your subconscious to make eating appropriately and working out a healthy diet the natural and automatic practices for you.

With the use of a professional hypnosis session, you can gain the motivation to adhere to your goals and actually enjoy pursuing and accomplishing those goals.

Any type of hypnotherapy product made to help you manage your weight has to attend to a number of ares of your life.

1. Your relationship to food.

2. Your relationship to exercise.

3. Your motivation or drive to achieve your optimal weight.

By dealing with these areas of your life it is feasible to transform your subconscious shows to show a much more healthy expectation. It then ends up being natural and simple for you to obtain your best body form.

You start to listen to the signals that your body naturally sends out to your mind and therefore start to collaborate with your body rather of versus it!

Weight Management Hypnosis

- Eliminate your cravings for unhealthy food while at the very same time conditioning your mind to delight in a healthy alternative.

- Engage in appropriate Exercise. This hypnosis imposes on the subconscious mind, a deep desire for healthy controlled exercise. This implies you will automatically desire to exercise and appreciate the entire procedure.

- Be motivated about your weight monitoring objectives. Being motivated to achieve your excellent weight is incredibly vital. If you can maintain it, almost any kind of good weight monitoring plan will work.

Unfortunately though many people give up before they see any type of real substance arise from their initiatives and swiftly slide back into their previous eating and exercise habits - often times their situation really worsens!

With the desire to consume healthy foods in the right parts, the all-natural feelings of enjoyment obtained from proper exercise and the inspiration to stick to your weight administration objectives you will certainly find it exceptionally easy to attain your purposes!

Hypnosis is not a "magic tablet" for weight-loss or weight management. Nonetheless, it is an extremely, medically backed, tool for changing the psychology of the mind. Without proper dietary limitations and exercise you will never ever accomplish your ideal weight.

It has been shown that to achieve weight-related (or any kind of) goals it is necessary to make adjustments in perspective and practices. This is where hypnotherapy succeeds. By altering your relationship to food and exercise, you can develop internal changes in yourself that make eating healthy foods and exercising properly things that you do normally and enjoy doing.

How to Train Your Brain to Burn Fat Fast

Hypnosis has actually been purported to work very effectively in several different habit-breaking protocols and has certainly been promoted as a good drive for dieters.

If you are open minded and are ready to believe that the power of the hypnotic idea is real, and is going to provide you with a helping hand in your weight loss journey, you are much more likely to see it work. If you think that hypnosis works, and consequently go through hypnosis as a mechanism to assist you to lose weight, you are far more likely to lose weight than a doubter would be.

There are entire bodies of work appearing around this "biology of belief" concept that your inner inclination is the essential element to the success rate you will see when attempting therapeutic treatments of any kind.

As part of a good dietary routine, and in a supporting function, if you believe that a good hypnotist can implant in your "inner ear" a suggestive incentive to follow through on your diet, by all means, do it! If you believe that just investing a couple of hours under the watchful-eye of the best mental magician is going to melt off the 20 pounds you've gotten for a long time, well, you are going to be bitterly dissatisfied.

You do need to select a great diet plan also! With that said, if you are a believer in the absolute power of the mind, go for it.

Bridging the Gap to Success.

Hypnosis and weight-loss are successful pair. Whereas lots of people try to tackle slimming down on their own, merely through self-discipline and motivation, and end up stopping work, weight loss hypnosis can supply the missing link that will eventually lead to success. By having the ability to soothe us down mentally by taking on the physical process that may be impeding our efforts.

One need to never think that it is their fault if they are not able to get down to their preferred weight. Hypnosis and weight loss are an obvious pairing that can tackle our subconscious to assist significantly in losing weight.

When you think about what is involved in the process of losing weight, using hypnosis for weight loss makes a lot of sense. In essence, we are breaking routines, behaviours, beliefs, and desires that we have held firmly for several years. Just thinking of dieting is enough to make anyone feel denied and, therefore, contributes to the level of difficulty that is being experienced. For that basic reason, it is crucial to discover a way to make the experience simpler and to find out a way to relax throughout the whole course of dropping weight.

Research study show that hypnosis, when used correctly, can have a considerable effect when used for weight-loss. A 9-week study of two weight management groups - one of which was executing hypnosis as a tool showed that the group that used hypnosis continued to show results more than two years later on. Adding hypnosis to any present weight reduction procedures you're currently doing, such as exercise and healthy eating increases your chance of dropping weight by about 97%.

Weight-loss is challenging, however weight gain is natural. Experts will inform you that diet plan and exercise is the only way to shed the undesirable pounds, but not everyone has the time to sign up with a fitness centre and the stress of life can lead to poor food choices. Hypnosis and weight loss can assist you in develop a more positive self-image. You will still be you, only better and healthier. Using hypnosis can help you feel more relaxed, and not just about food, but also in your day to day life. When you have the ability to conquer stress, you will no longer turn to food for comfort, therefore adopting a much healthier general mindset. Hypnosis can also help with positive thinking. You should never underestimate what a positive outlook can achieve.

CHAPTER FOUR

Gastric Band Hypnosis

The Gastric Band is a process of hypnosis used to change the lives of seriously overweight and obese people that have been unsuccessful at reducing weight using other techniques. It replaces the actual Gastric Bypass Surgery with a hypnosis-based different focused on achieving the very same result of reducing the quantity of food the stomach can take in one meal. While this sort of surgery of the mind is not new its application in the field of weight loss is new. Researchers over the world agree one of the keys to wellness, health and individual growth, depends on understanding the mind/body connection. Gastric band hypnosis is more secure and less pricey than having the equivalent surgery executed. It's also less dependent on how long you eat food and what you eat but the idea of smaller sections is instilled during the hypnotherapy sessions.

It requires several hypnosis sessions to not only cover the "setup" of the band but to modify actions of the individual. Many people distressed or squeamish about the idea of gastric band surgical procedure will be likely to assess one of these virtual stomach band hypnosis programs. The hypnosis techniques made use of need to be extra elaborate than a conventional hypnotherapy session. The gastric band "procedure" is taking place worldwide. What makes it different is it takes place in the subconscious mind. There is no operation, no cutting, no anesthetic as well as no recovery duration. The hypnotic suggestions are mostly placed in the subconscious mind which supports the body. The stomach will only hold a particular section of food.

How Gastric Band Hypnosis Works

Gastric band hypnosis makes use of the creative imagination instead of the scalpel to help overweight people restore control over their eating habits. You most likely already know what the stomach band surgeries or fat burning surgical treatments encompass. The procedure is executed in a medical facility operating space where a team of cosmetic surgeons and nurses make tiny incisions in your upper body and stomach as well as slide tiny surgical tools and electronic cameras right into your inner body. They cut and shed a tunnel around your stomach and also connect a banding gadget that can take off the top component of your stomach. The dimension of this top part of your stomach can be readjusted to make sure that it can be made to get just a little amount of food. So you end up being literally incapable of eating more than 4 or 5 mouthfuls conveniently.

As soon as this surgery is done, if you were to eat more than your new smaller b can hold, you will become physically incapacitated. This is a usual outcome that is called "dumping". It is so common that a word was created to describe the feeling. The reason for the surgical treatment is to make it compulsory for you to consume smaller sized amounts of food. Smaller meals will imply greater weight management. However there isn't assurance that you will consume smaller sized dishes, even if you have had the procedure. And there are times when those who have had the procedure have actually overeaten and triggered more issues to themselves due to the fact that their inner organs were changed.

This new weight loss program, gastric band hypnosis, takes advantage of on the imagery of the surgical treatment. Using your creativity, you will be persuaded that you have had the band dental implanted and you will respond as if you in fact have had the procedure. By using the power of your mind, your stomach will feel smaller and you will find yourself eating smaller amounts of food a result. Leaving you with the capacity to build the brand-new routines that will certainly sustain your new much healthier way of life for the remainder of your life.

Lately, Gastric Band hypnosis continues to be producing waves in the multimillion pound weight reduction organization, marketing itself as the technique that is ground-breaking to help people lose weight and also maintain their undesirable pounds away. Individuals have actually stirred up be they common homemaker to widely known stars using hypnosis for weight decrease way to preserve their bodies and also to help their fat loss. Like many new strategies in weight reduction, individuals ask is fat reduction with Gastric Band hypnosis an over-hyped dream that actually does not work-like marketed or can it be actually be the wonder that individuals have been looking for?

To a lot of individuals, the term hypnotherapy regularly evokes pictures of women as well as men performing ridiculous methods below a hypnotherapist's trainings. As a result of this portrayal of hypnosis, individuals occur to be slow to try and also skilled Gastric Band hypnosis as a weight reduction technique for his/her weight loss goals. An effective Hypnoband prepare for weight decrease differs from your standard method used by lots of Hypnotist, it is tailored at people with a BMI of over 25, not just a couple of extra pounds to lose.

Throughout a Hypnoband strategy, a weight reduction qualified Hypnotherapist might originally acknowledge what are the targets which you have for your self, they will clarify if these are possible and sensible. This phase is crucial as it determines targets which you are assured of getting to and also they get you to consent to these. Hence, by exercising a weight loss objective that you will be not uneasy with, you sub-conscious become more accepting of the target.

Supplying you with concepts that advertise better consuming as well as exercises, qualified hypnosis counsellors might additionally call for one to place in location a program on your very own. Viewing enhancement during your weight loss strategy further pushes one to continue to be on course to achieve the weight management targets you've established for on your own and also may form a positive-feedback cycle.

The actual hypnotherapy takes place over 4 meetings of around a hr, with normally a gap of around a month at the end to see the adjustment is developed and to give a booster on the rare occasions this is needed. In fact, it has been made use of in many components of the world successfully and is efficient and risk-free alternative to surgery and also is used with people who would receive stomach band surgical treatment as a result of the BMI.

For that reason, Gastric band hypnosis is authentic and also is presently aiding people from all profession with their weight decrease objectives. These are attained by them and also providing control in their way of livings providing a easy as well as fast means to obtain their wanted quantity of health.

Drop Weight With Hypnotherapy Using Gastric Band Hypnosis

Have you become aware of gastric band surgical treatment? People try it as an excellent way to shed weight and it does work to ensure but did you understand that it is a costly strategy and also one that is susceptible to issues like obtaining a slipped band, indigestion, irregularity, looseness of the bowels, queasiness and also throwing up and many others?

What happens if you found a way to have every one of the benefits without the danger and expenditure of the surgery?

There is a technique in hypnosis that offers this. Gastric band hypnosis is a new technique in hypnosis where you get ideas that you have had the treatment and incredibly you will start to act and live as if it were real. This is one of the several ways in which you can slim down with hypnosis.

Due to modern life and the ability to have any kind of food anytime you want, the majority of people lug extra fat. Two basic types of fat are common in your stomach. The first type covers your abdominal muscle mass and if you shed it your muscular tissues will be visible and you will get that torn appearance. It is called subcutaneous fat and is stored straight under the skin and over your abs. The second type of abdominal fat is called natural fat. Natural fat goes deep into your abdominal area under your muscular tissues and as a matter of fact, it surrounds your organs. This makes it specifically dangerous and while both raise your risk of diabetes mellitus, high blood pressure, stroke, and pressure illness, natural fat places you at a much better risk. This kind of fat is accountable for what is understood as a "beer stomach." Natural fat also launches more inflammatory particles into your body. It took a lot of added calories consumed over a very long time to get this fat accumulate so you can not anticipate it to come off easily and this is why some people take the phenomenal procedure of stomach band surgical treatment to put part of their belly out of order. This is an extreme action as we have actually seen, now Gastric Band Hypnosis can generate the very same outcomes without the surgical treatment component. With Gastric Band Hypnosis, a therapist will cause a trance and provide you ideas that will trigger you to think and act as if you have really had the procedure. This is a secure and effective way to lose weight with hypnotherapy.

CHAPTER FIVE

Hypnosis Techniques

- **Relaxation strategy**

Why do therapists ask to "make yourself comfy" and provide a soft leather couch to put down on? It's more than a typical courtesy. A relaxation is a typical approach used by therapists and a novice hypnosis method. They are most likely to speak with you and be open to indirect recommendations. Here are some common techniques of relaxation:.

- Make yourself comfortable.
- Set.
- Count down in your head.
- Controlled breathing.
- Relax & tense muscles.
- Speak in a soft tone.

Handshake strategy

Milton Erickson, the dad of hypnotherapy, is famous for using the handshake method as a method to cause hypnotic trance. Handshakes are the most typical type of greetings in our society. The handshake method shocks the subconscious by interrupting this typical social norm.

Eye Cues.

There are two spheres of the brain. One controls the "imaginative," which is the conscious part, and the other controls the "practical" known to be the subconscious. Always focus on the speaker's eyes as he/she communicates. Are they acting to the right, accessing the mindful, or the delegated the subconscious?

- **Visualization.**

Think of every detail in that space: the flooring, the shape of the windows, the painting on the wall, the smell, the light. Then, move onto a space they are less familiar with. As they have a hard time recalling the specific information, they open the mind to the idea.

- **Arm "Levitation" Technique.**

With this timeless Ericksonian method, the client begins by closing their eyes. The hypnotherapist makes ideas regarding the feelings in each arm. For example, they may say the arm feels light or heavy, hot or cold. The client goes into a trance and may physically lift their arm or they may simply believe in their mind that they have actually lifted the arm. In either case, the induction succeeded.

Hypnotizing A Person With Arm Levitation.

- Sudden Shock/Falling in reverse.

Continue with caution! Comparable to the handshake technique, a subject is finding themselves stunned can participate in a trance. I would never promote triggering any physical pain to a topic, but Erickson once demonstrated this by stepping on a female's foot and following it with an idea. A milder difference would be the "trust falls" that you may have heard of or took part in at a group structure event. The experience of falling backward shocks the system and opens the mind to a recommendation.

- **Eye Fixation**.

Have you ever discovered yourself "zoning out" and gazing at a fascinating item in the space while someone is talking? Did you entirely miss what they've started? You may have been in a hypnotic trance.

Any object of concentration can be used to induce trance. One can use a pendulum watch. You're more most likely to experience and stop working resistance using these items, due to their track record.

However, there are two secrets behind eye fixation. The things keeps the conscious mind occupied, opening the subconscious to recommendation. Secondly, the eyes tend to get physically tired when they moving back and forth.

Example: Try looking at the ceiling for a couple of minutes (without bending your neck). The eyes naturally tire and start to close.

- **Countdown Breathing.**

You might have become aware of regulated breathing for meditation, however, it can also a simple type of self-hypnosis.

- In an upright position, the arm should be on the lap, and eyes must be closed.
- Exhale air out through the mouth as you take deep breaths through the nose.
- Count down slowly from 100.
- Each exhales counts as one interval.
- In the end, you may think
- Remain in a trance. If not, continue the workout counting down from a greater number.

A recommendation is the wanted habits to be carried out by the customer. Post-hypnotic ideas are delivered after a hypnotized individual enters a trance, a state in which they are more open up to affect.

Erickson was a champ of indirect ideas. This technique puts the control in the subject's hands instead of those of authority, appreciating the patient's limits and clinical principles. It has proven more reliable to topics that are doubtful or resistant of trance.

Direct Idea

In conversational Hypnosis, a direct idea is an explicit command to carry out a specific action. Though effective, it is sometimes considered as dishonest because as the authority (a physician or hypnotist), you hold power over the customer. The customer does not control the choice to change habits with this method.

Here are some classic direct suggestions:

- " You will go to sleep."
- " You will stop smoking cigarettes."
- " You will drop weight."

- **Voice Tone**

The tone of your voice is especially beneficial when making ideas. This can double up with other strategies (like relaxation).

"You might wish to become unwinded."

In the above example, the word "unwinded" is spoken softly and extended. You can make a direct recommendation loudly, on the contrary.

"You will stop smoking cigarettes!"

Another perfect set for voice tone is the confusion technique. The therapist might change the tone of voice from whispering to screaming, talk with a different accent, or use a lisp, to puzzle the subject.

- Hypnotic trigger.

There are many forms of hypnotic triggers. A trigger advises the subconscious of a preferred action or feeling which was recommended under Hypnosis. Here are a few examples:

- Opening eyes.

- Sound of a bell.

- Snap of fingers.

- A clap of the hands.

- Standing or taking a seat.

- Opening a door.

Reading Body Movement.

- Nonverbal Communication.

Hypnotists are experts at nonverbal interaction, from reading a customer's body movement to communicating your own non-verbal tips. While a client might be saying something purposely, the subconscious mind could tell an entirely various story. Below are some examples of how the subconscious might impact body language:

- Facial expressions.

- Body posture.

- Voice tone.

- Pacing.

- Eye motions.

- Arms crossed.

- Head nods.

- Covering the face.

Become An Expert In Non-Verbal Interaction (with case example).

- Cold reading.

You may have seen psychics, mediums, phase therapists, or mentalists perform a "cold reading" on television for home entertainment works. Here's how cold reading works. If the topic is not smiling, the therapist might ask:

H: "Are you unhappy?"-- Start by asking a general or unclear concern from observation.

S: If they respond no, reset and ask another unclear question.

H: "Has somebody left you?" Drill down and ask a more particular question. This might be a relationship or a pet or a member of the family.

S: "Yes! How did you understand my feline fluffy passed away?".

- Warm reading.

With a warm reading, you make a declaration that could apply to anyone:

" You rejoice when you are surrounded by good friends."

- Hot reading.

The most challenging type, because you need to have some anticipation about the individual. Let's say their family member called you and told you that the individual was associated with a terrible time. When you fulfill them, you may concentrate on using the "regression to a cause" strategy since you have an idea about the past event.

- **The Swish Pattern.**

Submodalities are a neuro-linguistic program strategy used to dissociate the client or associate with a particular behavior. The five senses method involve (taste, odor, sight, touch, hearing), but submodalities is a subset the senses. Which are:

- Dark space.

- Bright or dim?

- Small or large?

- Color of white and black?

- Soft or loud sounds?

The Swish Pattern starts with visualization. When the client is in a trance, the hypnotist recognizes a couple of submodalities (brightness, size, etc.). The unfavorable action is big, focused, and bright in the foreground, while the necessary action is visualized as little and dim in the background. In the time it takes you to state "Swish" (the approach's name), the desired image rapidly becomes intense and big in the client's mind.

- Misdirection.

We see misdirection used in the real-life, often daily from politics to entertainment. The prefix "mis" implies wrong, and "direction" is connected to it, implying the audience is being led in the wrong direction. There are two types of misdirection one is literal, and the other is of the mind.

A simple demonstration of the very first would be a magician distracting people by waving a wand in his left hand and then performing a deception with his right. While the audience is misdirected, the magician slips a card up his sleeve, providing the impression that it has "vanished."

- Misdirection can likewise be a visualization:

"As you end up being nervous, picture yourself unwinding on a beach".

Here, a subject handling anxiety is misdirected to the visualization of themselves on a beach. The therapist has directed them from an undesirable image towards an enjoyable one.

- Reframing.

Usually done as a metaphor, reframing permits you to change the understanding of an experience in the customer's mind. For instance, imagine you have a client that wishes to reduce weight. They remain within and play computer games throughout the day. You could ask them to explain the procedure to "level up" their character in the computer game, what they do, how long it takes, how strong the character is at the start. And then, "reframe" the process of slimming down in their mind by comparing it to the computer game.

- **Regression to cause.**

The client enters a deep hypnotic trance where they can experience occasions as if they were really there (also understood as somnambulism). The therapist uses visualization to develop an "affect bridge" where the customer experiences an event for the first time again. The moment the hypnotherapist discover the cause, he can then find a suitable solution.

- **Anchoring.**

When we tape-record a memory, all of the emotions and senses are associated. These are "anchors" in your memory. Possibly the person has anchored the habits of cigarette smoking with a break, meal, sex, chatting with buddies, and other satisfying feelings. The hypnotherapist can suggest new anchors for more desirable behavior.

CHAPTER SIX

Mindful Eating: Foods To Avoid

Frequent studies indicate that healthy food consumption is an essential part of fitness programs. Some physicians teach healthy eating and lifestyle habits as a way to improve overall health by reducing obesity and related diseases. Below are some points that state the important of eating right to keep fit.

Food Is Our Medicine

Nutrient-dense foods, or' superfoods,' contain lean proteins, nutritious carbs and fats essential for our safety. A rich origin of vitamins, minerals and antioxidants is Superfood Antioxidants have been shown to reduce inflammation in our body, helping us fight disease. It is said that inflammation is the leading cause of many diseases. Powerful antioxidants in leafy greens and vegetables, for example, help to detoxify the body by removing harmful chemicals.

Many superfoods produce compounds that increase our metabolism to make fat burning more effective. Red peppers produce a molecule named capsaicin that has been shown to increase the rate at which we lose body fat.

Boost The Metabolism

Your best fat burner will not come in a tube, but by eating foods containing such compounds. According to research on nutrition, we can increase the rate at which we naturally burn fat by eating healthy. Eating foods that promote and improve the cycle of fat burning can help us lose fat more effectively. Adding food boosting metabolism will be a great complement to your existing workout and nutrition program. The following products are shown to improve our metabolism:

- warm peppers (active component capsaicin)
- Green tea (active component caffeine)
- Black coffee (active component caffeine)
- Cold water (500 ml of liquid per day improved metabolic rate by 30%)

The benefits of proper nutrition are the same as exercise, making a great recipe for good health!

When it comes to weight loss, what you're doing counts, obviously, you need to restrict calories in your diet to lose weight, but not all calories are equivalent. Sugar calories facilitate the accumulation of fat and appetite.

Have you ever attempted to relieve your appetite with a candy bar, just to get hungry again a short time later and crave more? Calories from fat and protein can help you feel full longer. Another way to approach healthy nutrition is to adopt a Mediterranean diet that has been shown to promote good health. The Mediterranean diet relies on meat from plant sources (fruit and vegetables), rice, whole grains, low-fat and non-fat milk, fish and poultry, nuts, seeds and olive oil, while limiting processed foods. When you adopt a Mediterranean-style diet, you'll consume more low-calorie-dense foods.

Now that have read this, we'd advise you to fill your tummy with some of food that will help you look fit and build your body. Constant exercise is essential, but according to research, eating right has the most significant impact on our fitness.

To eat right, there are a couple of guidelines that you can adhere to every day and they're not going to deny you of the foods that you enjoy, but deal with those foods as deluxe items, so you enjoy them more.

- Eat fresh vegetables and fruit that have high water content.

These are foods like tomatoes, watermelons, melon, kiwi, grapes etc. Every one of those fresh and flavourful, juicy fruits and veggies are excellent for you. These items have about 90 to 95% water, so you can eat a whole lot of these, and they will certainly fill you up without adding the pounds.

- Eat fresh fruit as opposed to refined fruit.

Anything that is refined has more sugar. Refined, and canister fruits additionally do not have as much fibre as fresh fruits.

- Increase your fibre consumption as much as you can

This implies eating a lot more veggies and fruits to repair your body tissue.

- Veggies are your friends when it involves shedding pounds.

There are lots of alternatives right here, and you may even intend to try some you haven't had in the past. When you can, the leafy environment-friendly varieties are the finest, and you always desire to work. Salads are loaded with much nutrients as long as you don't load them with many kinds of cheese. The leaves have a great deal of all-natural water.

- Be smart about what you consume.

Do not eat just to consume. Animals consume on instinct; people eat when they know their body indeed requires it. Don't be an impulse eater.

- Watch every little thing you take in from the food itself to what you top it with.

Condiments and garnishments can screw up a healthy and balanced meal since they are typically high in fat.

- Manage your craving for sweets.

This doesn't suggest you can not have your sweets; just don't consume them as a meal. Always keep in mind that these desserts end up.

- Set meal times and stay with them.

Ensure to have your meals at specific times and eat them at that time. A consuming pattern will help you to manage when you consume it. It is far better to have five small dishes a day instead than simply one or two massive dishes. Simply eating once daily makes your body feel as though it is deprived, which packs on fat as opposed to using it as fuel.

- Eat just when you are hungry.

Make sure to consume a glass of water first to start. Many individuals have the propensity to eat when they see food. It does not mean they are hungry; they just want to eat it. Do not consume anything you're used unless you really are starving.

When you're drinking water, you consume much less because you won't feel as though you are starving to fatality. Do not eat just to consume. An eating pattern will certainly help you to control what you eat and when you consume it.

- Try not to snack between meals.

However, if you should have a snack make sure it is a healthy one. If you take a trip a lot, look for healthy snacks and not processed food.

- Veggies make wonderful treats.

They can obtain you with the hunger pangs if you have them. Carrots are fantastic since they satisfy the appetite and they are loaded with nutrients.

- Counting calories is a good idea

If it is a packaged food item, after that it will certainly have the calories on the product packaging. Be sure to pay attention to offering dimensions in terms of calories. This is where food manufacturers get complicated, and you can fall to their catch.

- Avoid fries, it should be baked.

Fried foods are involved in fat and oil. Even after the unwanted oil has been drained away, there is still oil absorbed into the food item itself.

- Don't miss meals

You need to have, at least three meals a day, yet ideally five tiny dishes. This will keep you from obtaining hungry throughout the day and overindulging out of hunger.

- Don't consume more than one egg daily.

It is best if you can lower your egg consumption to 3 a week.

- Try to consume breakfast within an hour of waking up.

This is the very best way to prepare your body ahead of the new day. Do not wait up until you are starving.

- Your diet must consist of all facets of the food teams consisting of carbohydrates.

Actually, your diet regimen needs to be 50-55% carbohydrates. Carbohydrates are an excellent source of energy. Those diet regimens that restrict carbs are damaging you and only making you crave them that a lot more.

- Proteins must comprise only 25-30% of your diet.

Meat should be considered even more of a side meal as opposed to the main dish.

- Fats should compose 15-20% of your dish.

This amount is going to be in your diet plan as a kind of cream, sugar and so on.

- Eat white meat than red meat.

White meat includes chicken and fish. Red meat includes beef and pork.

- Try to go vegan as much as you can.

This truly is a healthier way of life, also if you can not reduce meat completely. The more fruits and veggies you can consume the much better. The more meat you eliminated, the much more fat you are leaving behind.

- White bread is excellent, however high fibre multigrain bread is better.

These breads include even more fibre to your diet regimen, and they additionally have a great healthy protein level.

- Pork does not assist in weight-loss by any means.

The less pork you consume, the much better off you will be when trying to reduce weight. Don't worry regarding dishonesty; however, don't cheat on a meal.

- Take it very easy on the salt and cut fifty percent of it.

Salt is among the major reasons of weight problems.

Burning up the Calories

To keep your weight continuous you have to maintain an equilibrium in between the power you eat food calories and the energy you use up for a physical job, so you can balance your weight. In warm weather, it's a great idea to take an additional walk daily or preferable go for swim instead, which is an excellent type of exercise.

The crucial point is to enhance your level of daily tasks. A few minutes of exercise daily helps to tone your muscles and enhance your stance and deportment, however, unless you genuinely work fairly tough for 1/2 hour they have no substantial result on your power balance. No slendering project is complete without the help of exercise. It tightens up slack muscles, tones the body, and leaves you feeling healthy and dynamic. More significantly, it helps you to keep that low level of weight you've worked so hard for.

Fats: Extreme amounts of fat in the diet can cause health issues. It is vital to have small quantities of fat in your diet because your body requires essential fatty acids to work appropriately.

Their chemical framework identifies fats, they can be filled, polyunsaturated or monounsaturated as well as the majority of the fat that you eat should be monounsaturated

A diet having high saturated fats can trigger your body to generate even more cholesterol, which might add to your threat of establishing cardiovascular disease and also some cancers. Saturated fats are mainly located in fatty meat, butter, full-fat milk items, cream lard as well as lots of takeaway and processed foods. They are additionally discovered in some plant food, such as hand or coconut oil. Select meat that has been trimmed of and lowered fat milk products, especially if heart problems are common in your family. All kinds of fat are abundant sources of power. There are around 27 kilojoules of energy in each gram of fat that you consume. Your body will certainly save any kind of excess calories eaten as body fat, which can cause obesity.

Sugars: Most individuals enjoy pleasant food, and also aside from sugar's effect on oral health and wellness, it is almost as dangerous to wellness as fat. Many foods having high sugar are likewise high in fat, so eating pleasant foods can result in high-fat consumption.

Sugar is included in small amounts to make valuable processed foods, and also these items need not to be excluded from your diet. High fibre morning meal cereals, as well as food such as canned baked beans, are nourishing, reduced in fat, and high in fibre and serve foods to include in a healthy and balanced diet.

Processed foods commonly have huge quantities of sugar included in them during processing. In the course of digestion, sugars such as sucrose and lactose and other carbs, such as starch can harm the body when it is in excess.

Salt: Salt has several purposes and also it escalates the natural flavours, colour and structure of foods. Our body needs percentages of salt to operate because it is a crucial nutrient that the body can not make by itself. Nevertheless, when salt is consumed in excess, it can raise your danger of developing high blood pressure. The National Health and also Medical research study Council recommends 1 teaspoon of salt each day. Also, if you don't include salt to your food, you might obtain this quantity of salt from eating produced food like potato pies, sausages as well as crisps.

Caffeine: Many people are addicted to caffeine. Tea, coffee, delicious chocolate, cocoa, and some soda pop beverages include caffeine.

Caffeine stimulates your mind and also the nervous system, and different physical results, vary from one person to another. These effects consist of enhanced performance, high heartbeat, and urinating more.

Some researches have actually revealed that high levels of caffeine can somewhat elevate blood pressure, whilst other studies have actually discovered reduced blood pressure in people that eat high levels of caffeine. There is no scientific proof to recommend that caffeine-containing beverages trigger particular issues if these are consumed in small amounts.

To help, keep an appropriate level of high levels of caffeine in your diet, restrict your high levels of caffeine intake to less than 600mg daily, this would certainly be 2-4 ordinary toughness mugs

Beverages that help in keeping you sharp, such as Red Bull include about 2 1/2 times the amount of caffeine discovered in regular cola beverages. If you are limiting your high levels of caffeine consumption, avoid these sort of beverages. There are numerous caffeine choices on the market.

Food Additives: Preservative is included in foods for a particular objective and is not taken into consideration to be food themselves. The human-made sweetener aspartame is added to numerous beverages, yoghurt, eating gum and various other food to keep the calorie content of the product low. Some additives help to keep or improve the top quality, colour, preference, and also texture of food and prevent them from spoiling.

- **GI**

GI means Glycaemia Index, which is a ranking from 0-100 that informs you whether a carbohydrate food will increase blood glucose degrees dramatically, moderately, or just a little. It offers you a step of how a carbohydrate will certainly impact your blood sugar.

- **Oil**

Choose poly or mono-unsaturated spreads anywhere possible, search for salt-reduced varieties. If you are trying so much to lose weight, a reduced-fat spread with just 50% fat will certainly help. If you have high cholesterol, think about a sterol spread such as sensible or Pro-active. They can aid in minimizing your cholesterol degrees if consumed in the amount suggested.

- **Saturated Fats**

It is the best idea to avoid these kinds of fats, which are found in butter, fatty meat, cheese, and also oils used in fast food. Rather switch to monounsaturated or polyunsaturated oil. Choose from sunflower, safflower, soybean, olive, and peanut or canola oil and stay clear of saturated oils such as coconut and palm.

Reduced G.I Foods consist of carbohydrates that slowly release sugar right into the bloodstream. This is optimal for those slimming down and also diabetics.

Tips to decrease your fat intake

Grilling as opposed to frying: Use a shelf filled with a little water when barbecuing, cooking, or roasting meat. Season lean meat in a mixture of soy sauce, white wine, natural herbs, garlic or spices. These will certainly protect against the meat from drying while barbecuing.

Steaming: Is an excellent means of cooking most veggies? The food is swiftly prepared using the vapour and also does not need any type of fat.

Microwave: Microwaving oven is a great method for cooking. The microwave allows foods to keep their flavour as well as wetness while they prepare.

Stir Fry: Make use of a frying pan or non-stick frying pan. Make use of a spray-on oil, red wine, stock, or water to fry your vegetables and after that quickly mix in your lean prepared meat.

- **Baked Vegetables**

Parboil veggies, spray with veggie oil, place in a dry pan, and chef in a stove on high up until crisp.

- Butter

Include reduced-fat yoghurt or ricotta cheese to vegetables.

- Cream

Replace cream with vaporized skim milk or blend skim milk with ricotta cheese.

- Instead of frying in oil, try cooking instead.

Cooking does not require all the fat and oil that frying calls for and your food is not taking in those substances while it cooks.

- Non-stick pans don't call for a lot of oil, so use non-stick pans.
- Boil vegetables rather than preparing them.

You can likewise steam them, as this is most likely the healthiest way to consume foods like cabbages, cauliflower, broccoli and carrots.

- Be cautious of no fat and reduced-fat food products.

There are a lot of these food products in the marketplace, yet they are not exactly healthy and balanced. Much of these food items make use of some sort of chemical or carb to sweeten them so that they taste better. The body turns these chemicals and carbs into sugar, which indicates they are still obtaining turned right into fat.

- Ensure you chew your food for about eight to twelve minutes

When food isn't correctly consumed and is just ingested, you load your tummy with food that isn't all set to be absorbed and after that it does not generate the wellness that you require.

- Ensure you use Extra Virgin Olive Oil when cooking.

It is extra expensive than other oil, however, the health and wellness advantages are far better, and it deserves the cost. Olive oil has been related to a reduced danger in coronary cardiovascular disease. It helps to raise the flexibility of the arterial walls, which lowers the possibility for cardiac arrest and stroke.

Controlling your Food Caving

Over 90% of men experience food yearnings. Below's a checklist of how you can efficiently suppress food cravings:

1. Avoid consuming less than about 1000 calories a day. By eating less than 1000 calories a day you will be likely overlooking some appropriate food group that is healthy for your diet.

Attempt to spread out your calories throughout the day and aim for 1500-2000 calorie per days. Expand this 1500-2000 calories right into 5-6 little meals. This will certainly keep you satisfied and additionally maintain a healthy and balanced weight loss metabolic process throughout the day.

2. When you are having food cravings, try to create an emergency diversion. Transform on the ipod, listen to your favourite tunes, contact a buddy, do something you were postponing or go exercising. Being with buddies, listening to songs, and exercise are all wonderful methods to pass the time up until the craving is gone.

3. Get sufficient sleep! Studies at the University of Westminster has identified that a couple of sleepless evenings a week can raise and trigger your hunger by as high as 40%! If you are tired and find yourself grabbing coffee throughout the day, choose sugar-substitutes rather than real sugar. Anything is much better than high-calorie foods, even if you are tired.

4. Attempt the "STOP TECHNIQUE" when you prefer instant craving control. When you understand your having an unnecessary food craving, say it out loud to yourself" STOP"! Picture yourself being lean and fit.

5. Prevent stocking up on processed food at home.

6. When you have high food cravings and can't curb them, avoid being around plenty of snacks all times. Try to shift your concentration on other activities such as job, doing tasks around the residence, reading, listening to songs, or anything your enthusiastic about. If you change your emphasis, recognize that food yearnings are only taken place within the short-term. Use these techniques of craving control, make them a part of your everyday life, and you'll be fine in the long-run as you reduce your weight, and stay healthy.

Eating Well And Losing The Pounds

In eating right there a couple of pointers that you can adhere to every day and they're not going to deny you of the foods that you enjoy, but deal with those foods as deluxe products, so you enjoy them more.

•   Eat fresh fruits and vegetables that have high water content.

These are foods like tomatoes, watermelons, melon, kiwi, grapes etc. Every one of those fresh and flavorful, juicy fruits and veggies are excellent for you. These items have about 90 to 95% water, so you can eat a whole lot of these, and they will certainly fill you up without adding the pounds.

- Eat fresh fruits as different to refined fruit.

Anything that is refined has more sugar. Refined, and canister fruits additionally do not have as much fiber as fresh fruits.

- Increase your fiber consumption as high as you can.

This implies always consuming more veggies and fruits to repair your body tissue.

- Veggies are your friends when it involves shedding pounds.

There are lots of alternatives right here, and you may even intend to try some you haven't had in the past. When you can, the leafy environment-friendly varieties are the finest, and you always desire to work. Salads are imbedded with nutrients as long as you don't pour excessive dress on and load them with many kinds of cheese. The leaves likewise have a great deal of all-natural water.

- Be smart regarding what you eat.

Do not eat just for eating sake. Animals consume on instinct; people eat when they know their body indeed requires it. Don't be an impulse eater.

- Watch every little thing you take in from the food itself to what you top it with.

Condiments and garnishments can screw up a healthy and balanced meal since they are typically high in fat.

- Manage your craving for sweets.

This doesn't suggest you can not have your sweets; just don't consume them as a meal. Always keep in mind that these desserts end up.

- Set meal times and stay with them.

Ensure to have your meals at specific times and eat them at that time. A consuming pattern will help you to manage when you consume it. It is far better to have five small dishes a day instead than simply one or two massive dishes. Simply eating once daily makes your body feel as though it is depriving, which packs on fat as opposed to using it as fuel.

- Eat just when you are starving.

Make sure to consume a glass of water first to start. Many individuals have the propensity to eat when they see food. It does not mean they are hungry; they just want to eat it. Do not consume anything you're used unless you really are starving.

When you're drinking water, you consume much less because you won't feel as though you are starving to fatality. Do not eat just to consume. An eating pattern will certainly help you to control what you eat and when you consume it.

- Try not to snack between meals.

However, if you should have a snack make sure it is a healthy one. If you take a trip a lot, look for healthy snacks and not processed food.

- Veggies make wonderful treats.

They can obtain you with the hunger pangs if you have them. Carrots are fantastic since they satisfy the appetite and they are loaded with nutrients.

- Counting calories is a good concept

If it is a packaged food item, after that it will certainly have the calories on the product packaging. Be sure to pay attention to offering dimensions in terms of calories. This is where food manufacturers get complicated, and you can fall to their catch.

- Avoid fries, it should be baked.

Fried foods are involved in fat and oil. Even after the unwanted oil has been drained away, there is still oil absorbed into the food item itself.

- Don't miss dishes.

You need to have, at least three meals a day, yet ideally five tiny dishes. This will keep you from obtaining hungry throughout the day and overindulging out of hunger.

- Don't consume more than one egg daily.

It is best if you can lower your egg consumption to 3 a week.

- Try to consume breakfast within an hour of waking up.

This is the very best way to prepare your body ahead of the new day. Do not wait up until you are starving.

- Your diet must consist of all facets of the food teams consisting of carbohydrates.

Actually, your diet regimen needs to be 50-55% carbohydrates. Carbohydrates are an excellent source of energy. Those diet regimens that restrict carbs are damaging you and only making you crave them that a lot more.

- Proteins must comprise only 25-30% of your diet.

Meat should be considered even more of a side meal as opposed to the main dish.

- Fats should compose 15-20% of your dish.

This amount is going to be in your diet plan as a kind of cream, sugar and so on.

- Eat white meat than red meat.

White meat includes chicken and fish. Red meat includes beef and pork.

- Try to be a vegan as much as you can

This truly is a healthier way of life, also if you can not reduce meat out completely. The more fruits and veggies you can consume the much better. The more meat you eliminated, the much more fat you are leaving behind.

- White bread is excellent, however high fibre multigrain bread are better.

These bread include even more fibre to your diet regimen, and they additionally have a great healthy protein level.

- Pork does not assist in weight-loss by any means.

The less pork you consume, the much better off you will be when trying to reduce weight. Don't worry regarding dishonesty; however, don't cheat on a meal.

- Take it very easy on the salt and cut fifty percent of it.

Salt is among the major reasons of weight problems.

CHAPTER SEVEN

Positive Affirmations

Negative ideas have probably been drummed into your head. Negativity from others, including good friends, fathers, and mothers, as well as from yourself resulting from the codependent relationship you have or had remained in. You will desire to trade those negative thoughts for positive ideas. What you concentrate on will be your truth, just as what you fear you develop is a fact. The power to train your ideas to concentrate on the positive is within each of us. If you wish to change your truth, alter your beliefs

Start with something little. An affirmation pertaining to health, spirituality to self-confidence will assist you to focus on the excellent that you desire to produce. That alone will assist manifest positive thoughts into your life. Focusing on the positive message carried out in the affirmation a number of times a day will not only help you feel better by lightening your spirits, but it will assist you in concentrating on encouraging messages rather than negative. You will begin to think that not only do you value the good that you are focused on, but also that it will affect you as you clear and open the way for the good. Negative ideas might occur at first, but part of the affirmation process is to write down those ideas to help clean out the old and develop the brand-new.

You can learn to be that way towards others when you find out how to be your own best good friend and be accepting of yourself. You must like yourself and feel safe within yourself before you allow yourself to deal with others the same way.

You can develop the world you live in. Everything starts with your belief system. You should find methods to negate old beliefs and replace them with the opposite of the positive. Don't try to force ideas with mental determination. Think within your heart to what you've believed in the past and take a look at your life and where that belief has led you. Set questions to your old belief system, think in your heart that brand-new success will come and that it will lead you to a better place. New options and new conclusions will follow.

Affirmations are not there for you to overlook the issues that may emerge. They help you to surpass the old practices you have that focus your attention on the bad. It assists in acting as if the affirmation has already taken location. Keep the positive firmly in mind and act adoringly towards yourself. Surround yourself with caring pals and individuals. And be grateful for the things you currently have and the things that might not have manifest in your life. When they do manifest in your life, be as appreciative of them as you will be.

When it comes to the affirmation process, you must be disciplined. It will be easy to add up. However, once you see your thoughts be more excellent and positive manifest in your life, you will be glad you kept with it. Make a note of your goals. Think of them and the unique you wish to see daily. Read meditation books. End up being conscious of what you are providing power to. If it's not positive and what you want, change those thoughts so you can create the life you want.

How do they work?

Affirmations are merely declarations that we say to ourselves that are negative or either favorable. We use affirmations every day. These affirmations essentially come in the form of our self-talk or inner dialogue that constantly walks around in our heads.

The Workings of The Mind

When we enter this world, our brain is like one big sponge soaking up all the info that it is fed. The source of this info originates from all the circumstances and experiences we experienced has we mature towards adulthood. Our moms and dads, households, teachers, associates, and friends usually form our life experiences in the early years.

All this info that is being fed to us is transported through what we call our mindful mind into our subconscious or unconscious mind.

- The Subconscious- The Mind's Hard Drive.

Our subconscious is, without a doubt, the most powerful part of our mind. Then your subconscious is the tough drive of that computer system if you believe our mind as a computer system. It's the part of your mind which stores every experience, circumstance, feeling, and sensation, both negative and favorable that we've experienced throughout our lives.

One of the main advantages of all these saved details within our subconscious mind is to assist us in keeping safe from any risk.

A good example of that is when you were young, your interest resulted in you having a look at your environments, which typically checked the borders of safety.

In fact, this can be done reasonably quickly and rapidly, among the most effective ways of reprogramming the mind is through the power of affirmations. Affirmations are merely the positive and negative declarations you state to yourself every day. Inner thoughts and dialogue determine your kind of thoughts. What's more, it is those constant thoughts that have brought you to where you are in your life today. By altering those constant thoughts, the course of your life will immediately change.

Using affirmations is an incredibly powerful strategy to assist you in doing this. Before you use affirmations, you initially need to become a persistent observer of your thoughts. Unfavorable thoughts you need to alter that believed to one that's positive in that extreme moment when you observe yourself thinking self-defeating. Doing this right away will neutralize the unfavorable thought there and after that avoid it from taking hold and contributing to the rest of the trash you store within your subconscious.

The entire work of using affirmations is to encourage your mind that what you're consistently verifying is the reality. This might be tough initially, but like everything, the more you do it, the simpler it ends up being.

Your mind holds the essentials in attaining every desire possibility. You will start to take control of your life once you take control of your mind. Your fate is before you. Create the life you've constantly dreamed of through the power of affirmations.

The Law of Attraction and Power of Affirmations

Energy surrounds us every day, to attract certain things to you and your life, surrounding yourself with favorable affirmations is a terrific method.

Affirmations are powerful. We sometimes make simple declarations in either a positive or an unfavorable tone, for example, when there is something that we need to get done, we often state, "It's too challenging." That declaration in itself is an unfavorable affirmation.

How does it work?

We handle our lives according to our beliefs. Like for instance, we are well mindful that touching a live wire would get us electrocuted, right? Notice the belief system of a kid, which is not yet totally developed. He does not understand that touching a live wire might harm him. However, as soon as that he is notified about what touching a live wire might do, it amounts to the development of his belief system, and he becomes conscious that touching a live wire might get him electrocuted.

Beliefs are stored in the subconscious mind. That is why in some cases, even if you make favorable affirmations like, "I believe I could lose 20 pounds," it does not seem to work because unconsciously, you think that it is hard to do which is exactly what your subconscious mind would tell you after you state your affirmation.

- **Avoid Using The Future Tense**

When making your affirmations, use the present tense. Using something like, "I will become wealthy," your ending up being wealthy will always remain in the future. Instead, state, "I think I am a wealthy individual," or "I picked to prosper." What are the options that have carried out in the past? Do you know your present life is the outcome of the choices you have made before?

- **Get A Positive Disposition**

To bring in positive energy, use of positive declarations in your everyday discussions. You might also jot down positive affirmations, as this technique amplifies the power of affirmations. Instead of focusing on unfavorable things, attempt to see and appreciate the wonderful things that life needs to provide. There need to be something you can be appreciative of in your life, no matter how little it is. Concentrate on it and see larger things you can be grateful to come your way.

Manifesting your desires ought to be enjoyable and amusing. It is not something you need to be overly major about. Without having a good time while doing it, your strategies become less effective. Keep in mind that altering your personality and your way of thinking does not happen overnight. Determination is a virtue here. With the power of affirmations and your knowledge of the Law of Attraction, your desires can be obtained.

Action 1 Make a Realistic List Of All Your Negative Qualities-

Make a list of all that you view as your unfavorable qualities. You put down the negative elements that your good friends, household, and colleagues have informed you about containing. It's essential not to be judgmental as to whether you feel these elements of you are true or false. Be truthful, be reasonable, and be real.

When you have finished your list, try to find any repeating styles that may exist, such as 'I am undeserving'. Determining these recurring beliefs is the essential very first action to begin moving from your negative mindset to one that is more positive.

Action 2 Make an Affirmation List That Will Cover Your Positive Aspects-.

These are the beneficial affirmations that will assist you in overcoming your positive sides. These will be part of your everyday affirmations. They are strong statements that will help your resolve-and will be your primary steps to attracting more of the important things you desire in your life.

- Adopt power affirmation statements such as "I am cherished and liked" instead of "I'm deserving of this".

- Use a thesaurus and ask a buddy to add suggestions and inputs to your daily affirmations.

Action 3 Recite the Positive Affirmations Out Loud, Three Times a Day. -.

To enhance these affirmations, its important you do them routinely every day i.e., First thing in the early morning, in the afternoon, and the last thing in the evening.

As this will be helpful in adding more emotion and feeling into your declarations, if possible, try and recite your affirmations while looking at yourself in the mirror. Some perfect times to do this would be when you are doing a few of your morning routines, such as when you are shaving or for women, when you are putting on makeup.

Action 4 Seek the Help of a Partner Or Friend.

Ask a partner or buddy to recite your affirmations to you. This will assist even more in reinforcing your brand-new beliefs as it's likewise coming from an external source. On the part that you can not get a partner, then you can once again use your image in the mirror as we went over in action 3.

Let me repeat once again. Daily positive affirmations are powerful tools for modification, but recognizing the self-undermining and defeatist beliefs are essential if they are to have the greatest effect.

It does not hurt if you seek advice from a professional therapist if you still have difficulty with some concerns. The therapist will help you to clear out some ingrained concerns within you.

Additionally, think about mind fullness meditation. Practicing meditation for a particular time in day will help you identify deep-seated concerns. The power of favorable affirmation also implies the power to accept your weaknesses. Affirmations are an incredibly effective tool to establish a favorable attitude. Unfavorable thoughts consistently going through your mind can seriously undermine your opportunities of living a happier, much healthier, and effective life.

CHAPTER EIGHT

Reprogramming Your Mind With Hypnosis

In order to be a new person, you should first believe like the brand-new individual you wish to be. It's incredible how the mind works. I've been discovering how the subconscious mind works for some time now. I have checked out a lot of material, and I've been practicing some of the techniques to reprogram my subconscious mind. I'm always shocked by the outcomes.

The conscious mind is where thoughts are generated. It is the one you use to believe, make decisions and provide orders to the subconscious mind. The subconscious mind executes what the conscious mind says without questioning. Here is where you hold all your beliefs (including limited beliefs) and practices (what you do every day). Our habits and beliefs control our everyday life. Fortunately is if we change our limiting beliefs and our practices, we will alter our lives, so that shows we require to change or reprogram our subconscious mind. How can we do this?

The subconscious mind discovers through repeating and affirmations. By repetition, we have formed our routines and beliefs. We can implant new ones using the same method. If we desire to alter our life by implanting new beliefs and routines, the very first action we need to do is to know what we truly really wish to have, do, and be. When we understand that we will realize what routines and beliefs we need to replace or change to attract what we've always wanted.

It is essential to understand that the brain is formed by 4 phases: Beta and Alpha in the conscious mind and Theta and Delta in the subconscious mind. When we are completely awake, we are in the Beta. When we start to go to sleep, we are in the Alpha. When we are sleeping, we are in the Theta stage, and when we are deeply asleep, we reach the Delta state.

According to Sigmund Fred, we can access the subconscious mind when the brain remains in Theta state, so we can quickly imprint new beliefs or habits when we are in the Theta state.

Here are some methods for reprogramming the subconscious mind. The majority of these techniques include autosuggestion. Autosuggestion is a term that describes the process in which individuals stimulate their minds through repetitive ideas, images and/or words by self recommendation.

- Positive Affirmations.

Affirmations are positive statements, and empowering questions. A strong affirmation would be one composed in the first person (I), for example, "I feel very happy completing my task." An empowering question can be, "Why do I feel very excited now that I have finished completing my task?" I believe it is a good concept to add the word "now" in your affirmations. Often I like to use the words "I command" in my affirmations: "I command you to be healthy and feel excellent!" This works for me, too!

- Creating Visualization

Creative visualization is a mental strategy where you use your imagination to create what you want in life. You can assist yourself using a vision board, composing a script, creating a mind movie, or any other visual thing that works for you.

- Meditation assists you to clear your mind and increase your inner peace.

Meditation assists you to be mindful of your thoughts, so it might be simpler to reach your subconscious mind when you practice meditation.

Search for audio programs that are designed to reach the subconscious mind. This helps you to implant an affirmation, belief, or goal into your subconscious mind straight with no resistance. I've heard that some individuals feel exhausted, nervous, or have headaches after they begin to practice this approach. Personally, at the start, I experienced itching on my face and head, but now I feel fantastic! Some people recommend that you require to listen to the very same affirmations for at least ten consecutive days (30 days is best) to make them work. This is the only one of the approaches where you can reach your Theta state quickly, the state where you can access the subconscious mind. I like to listen to my affirmations throughout the day when I'm working, too. It helps me to meditate about them.

If you think you have limited beliefs or bad habits that are limiting your success, it would be much better to start with affirmations to help you to clean your mind. Ex. "All my worries concerning public speaking are leaving now from my mind." After you clean your subconscious, you can place brand-new beliefs into your mind, otherwise, your old beliefs can screw up the brand-new ones.

There are other approaches to assist you to reprogram your mind, like Hypnosis, subliminal videos, subliminal software application, EFT (Emotional Freedom Techniques), and more. Still, you will require some professional help, or buy them. You can work with the methods I've discussed on your own. You simply require to auto-evaluate yourself, perhaps do some research and try them to see what works best for you. Follow these steps:

1. Identify what you really want and what your minimal beliefs are if you have them.

2. Tidy your subconscious mind with your affirmations.

3. Insert new beliefs into your mind with positive affirmations.

4. Establish new routines through your actions.

Thoughts may influence the subconscious mind (words) blended with feelings and sensations. Through your feelings and emotions, you can alter your favorable vibrations and affect your subconscious more easily. That is why when you are wildly pleased, you can attract more things through your favorable emotions, you alter your vibrational state of mind to match the good things you are looking for. When you use words that link you with a positive feeling or sensation in your affirmations, you increase your chances to imprint them in your subconscious mind, so have fun with them!

All success originates from behaviors, and all habits begin as repeating of actions, thoughts, and words. When you change your core beliefs about yourself and life, you can be successful in whatever. Learn how to control the power and make use of your mind, and your life will be the one you have constantly desired. Have faith that you are worthy of a terrific life and believe every word (idea) that you are trying to implant in your subconscious mind. To be a beginner, you need to initially think, talk, act, and feel like the beginner you wish to be.

Enhance Your Ego With Hypnosis

The way to access those sensations is accessing and reprogramming the subconscious where they live. All ego-strengthening techniques do that at some time. For them to be effective, they need to target your "stream of awareness", much like when you talk to yourself, as we sometimes discover ourselves doing.

Some professions need more of a "difficult shell" than others. Sales clerks are often put through a lot of demanding circumstances, and they simply need to find out how to handle even the most difficult clients. Negative, self-defeating ideas still enter their minds, however they have trained themselves and are capable of deflecting them. With the help of self-hypnosis, they get the capability of stating "no" to an unfavorable though that's flying through their minds and choose to instead consider something more productive, or merely just do it. That's not an intrinsic quality, however, it can be found out. Yes, you may say it has something to do with positivism. That's the way things work. You require to control yourself first if you desire to manage your environment. Or your ideas, as is the matter.

Hypnosis does not break a person's will or morals.

So no, you can't hypnotize somebody and make them dedicate a crime. It won't work. Unless that individual is currently criminally oriented, and such a thing won't cross paths with their ethical compass. What Hypnosis can do, nevertheless, is offering power to much deeper will and desires.

 In essence, telling a person's subconscious (with the aid of hypnotic strategies) "not" to do something just won't work. It's more reliable to inform it what "to do", rather than "not to do". With a little bit of work, it can be deceived into acting more proficiently and, therefore, enabling an individual to work much better. A therapist has to target it in such a way that it keeps the client away from self-defeating patterns and program it to concentrate on productive thinking.

Eventually, the objective of strengthening your ego with Hypnosis is getting to a frame of mind when you can unwind and no longer worry a lot if your hair looks great or if your clothes are tidy etc. That, and getting an edge over intricate or difficult scenarios, rather than having your insecurities control you. The next time your mind talk with you, have it state the words of victory and not those of defeat.

How to Increase Your Metabolism With Hypnosis

How many people do you understand that can consume as much as they desire, however, they never appear to get any weight? When you appear to eat the same things, you put on weight? The person starts having a slow metabolic rate results. This can be altered with a combination of a correct workout routine (that primarily targets substance muscle groups), a healthy diet, and even with the use of Hypnosis.

Many individuals with slow metabolic rates discover it easy to put weight on. The effort added in losing the weight that is acquired is always far higher than getting it in the very first place. Can you imagine using a 100% natural method to raise this metabolic rate? This technique can permit you to reach your weight loss goals and keep that weight off in the long term. Hypnosis is a natural approach for attaining this. It is created to relax you into a state where your subconscious mind can be accessed. Once you have gotten past the guard of your rational and conscious mind, you can then begin to make changes to your subconscious mind. By merely increasing your metabolic it can assist you to attain the weight-loss you have always imagined.

By reprogramming your mind, you can optimize your metabolic rate. Ensure the food you eat is digested and processed both rapidly & efficiently. Taking control of your body's metabolic rate is among the keys to slimming down. Hypnosis can allow you to do this naturally and healthily.

For anybody who is searching for a fast solution to increasing there metabolic rate, you have pertained to the wrong location. This can not be done healthily and surely not naturally. However, with the use of Hypnosis, this can be attained gradually with practice. After the first few sessions, you will begin to feel the results that are associated with an increased metabolic process, which include an increased energy level and starting to feel more alert throughout the day. It will end up being more effective and rapidly break down food. Optimizing dietary stores and giving you the best energy readily available. Your body will stop keeping excess food that it might never break down in the past.

You will start to see the results in the mirror and on the scales, as you begin to slim down and condition. Gradually moving you closer to your perfect weight. It doesn't stop there! Having a quicker metabolic rate is the key to maintaining a healthy body. So it will be much easier to avoid putting the weight back on.

Stop Smoking with Hypnosis

The cigarette companies have actually been using psychology and hypnotic induction techniques to get you addicted to their products for lots of years without you even understanding it. The producers have been stylishly advertising an addicted product. As soon as you realize that, imagine how you would feel.

There is just one thing to do, take ownership of your mind for a change. Despite what anyone else informs you, it is your mind to do with as you choose. If somebody wishes to stay addicted to cigarettes, then that depends on them, but if you desire to stop cigarette smoking then we can assist.

In the next couple of days, you might discover your 'addiction' fading away. You see, the trick is not to attack that 'addicting program' directly this needs a substantial force of will as people use brute force to get their way. Even then, the unconscious program is still there, so cigarettes will always tempt people.

What you can do, however, is to change the source of the problem.

Reprogramming your mind with self-hypnosis is very easy to do, and all it needs is a CD or MP3 gamer. As you listen to these hypnotic programs they will oust that nasty 'addiction' and totally free your mind from the grasp of cigarettes.

You will no longer be a smoker or ex-smoker, however, you will be a non-smoker. Free to live your life healthy for a better change.

Reprogram Your Mind And Become Slim And Trim!
Are you trying to find a way to beat your yearnings and get slim without too much will power and hunger? You need to think about why exactly it is that you want to lose weight. Why? Merely because inspiration is the key factor in whether we reach the goals we set ourselves.

Not everyone wants to shed weight simply to look good, though for lots of this is their main motivation, specifically before a vacation in the sun! Some individuals picked to focus on ending up being slimmer when they find their life is being limited or limited in some method. How many of you have been mortified when you no longer fit in the size clothes you thought you were or discover that you are unfit and too obese to even take on the stairs to the hairdressers?

When we are forced to take a look at a problem that adversely affects our life in some way, such as being overweight, we are more than most likely going to decide then and there to do something about it. So we make a dedication to go on a diet plan.

Over 98% of all diets fail, with over 30% of dieters putting more weight on! And besides, the number of diet plans can you in fact state you have enjoyed? I could not believe anything more depressing than replacing diet plan anxieties and rejects for food! Diets play havoc with your blood sugar levels, which increases those cravings!

So if diets run out the concern, how are you going to shed that excess weight effectively? Well, you have one of the most effective 'computers' on the planet to depend on to help you reach your ideal weight. Your subconscious mind! This is the aspect of the mind that is accountable for your routines, behaviors, and how you feel and believe. So if you make changes at the subconscious level, by reprogramming your mind, you will find you reach your objectives a lot more effortlessly.

So how exactly do you go about reprogramming your mind for success? First and foremost, focus on what you need instead of what you don't want! How numerous times have you based on the scales and despaired at just how much you weigh or searched in the mirror groaning about how fat you are? Well here's the point - if you concentrate on being overweight and unattractive you will be fat and unsightly but if you focus on being slim and healthy, guess what! You will be slim and healthy.

Start right now and begin focusing on precisely what you desire in life (to be slim/healthy) as opposed to what you do not (fat/unfit/unattractive)! Look in the mirror and continually inform yourself you have a right to be slim and healthy! Hang up that dress in the size you wish to be and imagine how spectacular you will feel and look in it (and not how depressing it is that it does not fit you).

So focus on shedding weight, releasing excess weight, being slim and healthy.

144

Furthermore, your subconscious mind enjoys to keep you delighted so if you whack up those fantastic feelings of joy, wellness, pride, vigor etc whilst visualizing the new slimmer you, it will work even more to develop the image or goal you desire!

Positive affirmations can assist you to change a bad practice or behavior "I picked to take pleasure in eating healthily" or can help you reach a goal such as your ideal weight "I am slim and healthy". Notice how these affirmations are mentioned in today tense and not the future. This makes sure that you act now and not put it off till later. If you inform your subconscious mind, "I will be slim and healthy" when exactly is it that you desire to be slim and healthy? Five years from now?

Remember 'What the mind can develop the mind will achieve' so by envisioning yourself at your perfect weight and stating your positive affirmations typically throughout the day, as well as concentrating on what you desire in your life, you are helping to reprogram your mind to get what you want!

If you can reprogram your mind to produce this wonderful slimmer, trimmer, and much healthier you, your subconscious mind will produce new methods to help you change your existing bad consuming and way of life habits to healthier and more positive ones. You may simply discover that you begin to take pleasure in more activity while eating less and more healthily without the need for any will power what so ever!

Use Your Mind to STOP Emotional Eating

Why is it essential to understand the difference between Emotional Hunger and Physical Hunger? If you remain in the procedure of slimming down, starting a diet plan, or changing your way of life, then finding out how to recognize Emotional Hunger can be the distinction in between battle and success. Learning to recognize emotional hunger allows you to start the process of eliminating Emotional Eating.

If you do not consume food for several hours most likely, you'll discover yourself feeling starving. However, is it "genuine" cravings? Or is the sensation "emotional" hunger?

Can you remember the last time you felt starving? Did you see a feeling in your stomach, maybe a gnawing feeling, perhaps a rumbling type of feeling? If at the time you didn't take notice of that sensation by eating something, would that feeling grow bigger as time goes on?

You know what physical appetite feels like if this is a familiar sensation and one you might really identify the place on your body where you are feeling it.

The majority of people (possibly you) rarely experience this sensation. Many people tend to consume before they get hungry or consume when it's "time to eat", regardless of whether they feel hungry at the time.

In the past, if you were hungry, you probably would have to wait until you got home to eat. Now that there are many places to eat junk food at restaurants, mini shops at gas stations, and food sections in drug stores, it's rather simple to grab something while you are on the go. It may not be healthy, however, it will definitely be convenient.

Emotional Hunger is quite different from Physical Hunger. If you don't pay attention to it, physical Hunger comes on gradually and grows stronger. Emotional hunger however, begins quite rapidly. And emotional cravings is lack of that familiar feeling in your stomach.

In reality, Emotional Hunger normally comes on quite rapidly. Emotional Hunger begins as an idea "I really desire to eat something right now," or you may discover yourself in the cooking area thinking, "I wonder if there is anything good to eat around here." Often emotional hunger simply occurs when you stroll through the kitchen area, and you find yourself getting something to put in your mouth.

When the thought of eating comes into your mind quickly and is NOT accompanied by that feeling in your stomach, then you are experiencing Emotional Hunger.

Individuals who eat when they are physically starving and stop when they no longer feel starving tend to be healthy and trim.

When they experience Emotional Hunger tend to be obese, people who eat. Why? Emotional Hunger leads to Emotional Eating. And when individuals consume for psychological factors, they tend to continue up until another feeling surpasses the feeling.

Picture a female who is annoyed with her household. She feels the desire to consume even though she might not feel starving. She starts eating and consuming ice cream. Maybe chips, some cookies, and some leftovers. She may continue to consume till her stomach feels overstuffed, however, will this make her disappointment disappear? Obviously not.

Fact: no amount of food will ever satisfy any emotion.

A good guideline to follow is this: every time you bring food to your mouth, ask yourself, "am i hungry?" if you are not hungry, as yourself, "what am i feeling?'

If you don't understand what you are feeling, that's ok. Simply understanding that you are not hungry is a fantastic start. When you understand that you are not starving, you can stroll away from the food. You can pick to do something else. Read. Take a walk. Call a good friend. Do something you take pleasure in.

The most convenient way to reprogram your mind and alter your routines is to use the power of your subconscious mind, which is easily accessed with Hypnosis. The power of the mind can be used to achieve your goal is the guaranteed method of personal success.

CHAPTER NINE

The Power of Self-Suggestion

In this chapter, we'll review the power and impact of tip and self-suggestion (just how they're various and just how they connect to each various other). We'll take an appearance at the popular practices that use the power of suggestion as

types of self-therapy and discover their weaknesses as well as toughness.

Pointer and Self-Suggestion

The power of pointer plays an important role in the choices we make and the high quality of life we generate for ourselves. And also while I'm certain you've become aware of the power of recommendation, few people ever pause to consider what is implied by it. What is pointer? How and why is it thought about to be a resource of power? Right here's my definition:

A pointer is a suggestion or proposal developed to impact a feedback or evoke in thought or habits.

These propositions concern us from a range of resources and also in varied methods. There are exterior pointers, which can originate from places, things, or people. Any kind of time a person asks you to do something, it's a pointer. At any time someone regulates you to do something, it's merely a much more emphatic recommendation: it's up to you to abide. If your supervisor tells you to cleanse up the display screen situation, it's really just a pointer. If a costs is available in the mail with a need for payment, it's really a tip with an underlying essential. One more example of pointer at work would certainly be when you shop at the food store and also you notice an appealing photo on the frozen pizza box. That picture is an exterior recommendation designed to influ- ence (or seduce) you to acquire that item. Exterior ideas also come in the type of revealed info. Whenever a person tells you something regarding himself or herself, you're exposed to tips. Anytime you review anything, you're exposed to suggestions. This publication you're currently reviewing has plenty of ideas.

Self-suggestions, on the other hand, are concepts we suggest to our- selves, suggestions that start from our own minds. A great instance of a self-suggestion would be when you ask yourself what you seem like eat- ing for dinner. You quickly assume concerning various foods or foods and you make a decision based simply on your tastes and interior motivations when you ask this of yourself. Or to place it extra simply, you speak on your own into selecting what to have for dinner. Your life teems with this sort of interior discussion-- or inner self-suggestion. You make suggestions to on your own each day, and this should be plain enough to see with a little bit of understanding.

Your Mental Diet

Tips have a solid impact on your quality of life. I'm certain you've heard diet experts say "you are what you eat." They are claiming your physical condition is straight pertaining to your diet regimen. They contend that what your body digests and also takes in has a strong bearing on its capability to work. Pointers, by analogy, resemble food-- food for the mind. And also the pointers you take in on an everyday basis, whether from an exterior source or from self-suggestion, comprise what you may call your psychological diet plan. Every idea you subject yourself to, whether coming from the media, your friends and family, and even self-talk, comprise your psychological intake. As well as they can potentially have a significant effect on your emotions, mind, and also body.

Symptomatic thoughts can impact you as an outcome of abrupt or repetitive events. Each of these can influence you because of the thoughts they suggest and also the emotions they can evoke in you. Recurring occasions can likewise influence you.

Maybe none of us can forecast when unexpected occasions may take place or how they'll influence us. As well as it's up to us to choose what food for idea we're going to absorb as well as what we'll dispose of.

How Your Mental Diet Affects You

Your mental diet influences your psychic and also physical health. It needs to be apparent that if you subject yourself to negativity, your emotions and ideas are impacted. And if you do this on a regular basis, it is not hard to comprehend that you might be so deeply affected, you can become regularly fearful, angry, and negative.

Your body is additionally subject to the power of suggestion. You may question how your ideas can impact your physical body, as several of us think and act as though body as well as mind are separate.

Your mind is not an abstract island with a remote relationship to your body. They are inexorably linked. Are you surprised? When you think of a satisfied memory, your subconscious mind instructs your body to duplicate the physiological state related to happiness, including the excretion of the feel-good hormones called endorphins. When you view an activity flick your heart races along with the hero's. Your body responds to what you are believing to produce the physical indication of anxiety when you read a thriller novel. We view movies mainly so we can vicariously experience the tales via the personalities. But there is a physical consequence, since your subconscious stores every one of your psychological as well as physiological reactions in its memory for future recommendation. This does not have to be a poor point, certainly. A lot of the New Thought group disapprove watching a film with delights, experience, and physical violence of any kind. But it can be argued that the mind can make use of information of a relatively volatile nature in order to overcome individual issues. And while not specifically advocating physical violence in flicks, publications, or music, I am explaining that it may well give a way for some individuals to connect with deep internal problems and also hopefully start to settle them.

I also desire to make it clear that I'm not one of those gurus that will tell you never to think an adverse thought or that you must be positive no issue what your mood or circumstances. Just as when we eat too much of the wrong foods we can anticipate health problem and also illness to capture up with us, this is also true with thought junk food. We must discover a means to provide ourselves with healthy, uplifting recommendations to combat the negative ones.

Methods of Self-Suggestion

All of us involve in self-suggestion on a regular basis, though we seldom quit to analyze it. My mindsets and actions pertaining to chocolate cake may then end up being understandably erratic, so a structured method for delivering regular messages to the subconscious is required.

There already exist several (more or less usual) official or structured techniques of self-suggestion that have actually become prominent in recent times. The objective of all formal techniques of self-suggestion is to produce a strong impression on the subconscious, due to the fact that one point is clear when it pertains to self-communication:

If the subconscious continues to be unimpressed by our communiqués, our existing scenario and also patterns of idea and behavior are most likely to remain the same.

You might know with a number of organized types of self-suggestion. Self-hypnosis is a technique used to silent or bypass the mind's natural filter so reasonably direct interaction can take area in between the conscious mind and the subconscious. In this state, ideas for positive change are imparted from the conscious mind to the subconscious. Imaginative visualization is a method needing the participant to picture usually metaphoric and also details imagery to send messages and create an influence on the internal mind. This is usually executed in a very relaxed physical problem. Self-affirmations declare declarations regarding the self repeated over and over till their intent is soaked up by the sub- aware. All 3 of these techniques have their values and also downsides.

Let's analyze them briefly

Standard self-hypnosis is, without a doubt, a remarkable device for self-transformation. Not everyone is thrilled or comfortable with the entire altered states of consciousness thing, and it does take at least fifteen minutes to execute, which can be a difficulty to those with a difficult schedule.

Lots of people (if not most) find it impossible or challenging to aestheticize to any type of excellent level, so the potential power of the symbolic imagery is lost on them. It ought to also be kept in mind that if performed in a kicked back state, as it regularly is, this kind of self-suggestion is really a type of self-hypnosis in camouflage.

Self-affirmations are a fantastic suggestion externally and call for no modified state on the component of the expert. In real way, nevertheless, issues are generally experienced. For one, the outcomes are generally slow-moving in coming and also it takes rather a little bit of time and effort to repeat expressions dozens of times, day in day out. The concept of using regular rep to saturate the subconscious is a legitimate and effective one, yet it usually generates a state of boredom in the professional. And also affirmations provided in a state of boredom are most likely to be disregarded by the subconscious. As with imaginative visualization, when self-affirmations are executed in a relaxed state, it ends up being a form of self-hypnosis, which then owes its effects largely to the altered state.

The Ideal Self-Suggestion Method

From the above-mentioned methods, we can place together components required for an optimal approach of self-suggestion gave that it requires neither a modified state of recognition nor any kind of added time to implement, yet retains the powerful aspects of conventional self-hypnosis, visualization, and also affirmations. Such a technique would include:

Regularity of application.

We understand that the subconscious responds to normal actions and ideas a lot more conveniently than to the occasional. So it is crucial that our self-suggestion initiatives be regular and also relentless.

Evocation of positive and strong feelings.

When influenced by relevant and straightforward feelings, the subconscious responds well to self-suggestion. By positive emotion, it implies that the generated feelings must concentrate on the objective that you do want, instead of the bad or negative feelings that you may be attempting to get away from.

Application of ideal pictures and metaphors.

The old saying which is often repeated, "a picture tells a thousand words" applies significantly when it comes to communicating successfully with the subconscious. Plain action words without assigned images have little influence on surviving. By combining our words with ideal signs, allegories, and pictures, our designated guidelines are completely recognized by the subconscious.

The big question after evaluating every one of these optimal aspects is: Can such an ideal method of self-suggestion be devised? Yes! I call it Self-Hypnosis Revolution. It is very crucial to be aware of the number one requirement for the efficiency of any type of overt technique of self-suggestion, including the one you're trying to find out:.

You have to believe in the power of self-suggestion for it to work as expected. That is to say, you must wholeheartedly believe that your subconscious is prepared and eager to listen to and act on your favorable self-suggestions in whatever type you select to use them. Even more, you need to under- stand that the subconscious is then greater than with the ability of modifying your body, your actions, as well as even your circumstances to produce and also sustain wellness, happiness, success, as well as so forth. Even a slight shock or skep- ticism in the value of self-suggestion or the powers of the subconscious can be adequate to work as a counter-suggestion that can stop your success.

Please note; it is not that idea itself makes a self-suggestion strategy work well in the long term. That's because uncertainty and skepticism are proof of an inverted idea-- an idea that self-suggestion initiatives are of no value. And also that kind of belief acts as a psychological barrier and really protects against progress with any type of technique of self-suggestion, no matter how powerful its potential is.

CONCLUSION

A woman has the ability to build systems of her own nerve by doing the things she's generally averse to doing. Physical and intellectual guts are very essential, it is ethical guts that is especially important to a woman.

This happens to be one of the most essential aspects that separate the typical woman from the type of woman who leads others.

Remember to keep on learning and to continue on your own personal advancement path towards growing as a woman. Do this and the best man will see you as an irresistible catch; the kind of woman that he would rather not live his life without.

Before you go, I would like to say "thank you" for acquiring my book. I know you could have selected from dozens of books on the subject or focus of this book, however, you gambled on my book and for that I am highly grateful.

Thanks again for checking out all the information and knowledge provided in this book.

Made in the USA
Monee, IL
04 January 2023

24368601R00095